Version-Independent Programming

Code Development Guidelines for the Windows® Operating System

by D. James Benton

Foreword

This book presents a set of guidelines by which to develop applications that will run on any version of the Windows® operating system. This is not a manual on computer programming, but it does address the subject where necessary. The reader is presumed to be proficient in the C programming language, as this is the clear choice for such development. Simply put, this is a manual on what to do and what to avoid, in order to achieve version-independence. As more versions are released and the time between new releases is shortened, compatibility becomes increasingly important. By following these guidelines, the resulting applications will not only be compatible, they will also be more efficient. Version-independence is a specific type of performance. Achieving performance always requires attention to detail. If you are not willing to pay attention to detail, you will never achieve performance.

All of the code snippets contained in this book,
along with a lot of free software is available at...
https://www.dudleybenton.altervista.org/software/index.html

i

Table of Contents   page

Foreword i
Introduction 1
Chapter 1. What's Up with Compatibility? 3
Chapter 2. The Basics of Windows® Programming 7
Chapter 3. Objects and Controls 11
Chapter 4. The Secret to Version-Independence 33
Chapter 5. Working with BUTTONs 35
Chapter 6. Working with FONTs 39
Chapter 7. Working with LISTBOXes 41
Chapter 8. Working with PROGRESS Controls 43
Chapter 9. Working with SCROLLBARs 45
Chapter 10. Working with STATUSBARs 47
Chapter 11. Working with TABCONTROLs 49
Chapter 12. Working with TREEVIEWs 51
Chapter 13. Working with Clipboard Data 57
Chapter 14. Performing a Screen Capture 61
Chapter 15. Charts & Graphs 63
Chapter 16. Making it all Fit on the Screen 81
Chapter 17. Acronyms 85
Appendix A: C Compilers 87
Appendix B: The .Net Framework® 89
Appendix C: Visual BASIC® 91
Appendix D: Linear vs. Object-Oriented Code 93
Appendix E: 16-32-64-Bit Programming 95
Appendix F: Working with Very Long Path Names 97
Appendix G: Painting with a Mask 99
Appendix H: Put A Menu Wherever You Want It 101
Appendix I: Click Here to Do Something Special 103
Appendix J: BITMAPs with 32 Bits/Pixel 105
Appendix K: Using Command Line Parameters 107
Appendix L: To GUI or Not To GUI 109
Appendix M: Manually Loading a DLL 111
Appendix N: Painting without Flicker 113
Appendix O: Directory Walk 115
Conclusion: Attention to Detail Matters 119

Introduction

Many operating systems have been introduced since the invention of the computer, but none so successful or ubiquitous as Microsoft® Windows®. One of the unusual things about the Windows® operating system that is often taken for granted is the ability to run the same application on more than one version. This was also true of MSDOS®. Most other operating systems have required compilation and linking of each application for each version of the operating system as well as versions the application itself. When this is the case, the user must either have access to the source code or obtain an updated version of every application to accompany each new version of the operating system.

The ability to run the same application after migrating to the next version of the operating system–without having to purchase a new copy–has greatly contributed to the success of Microsoft®. This compatibility also reduces the potential revenue stream flowing to software developers. From the user's point of view, this has meant sustained utilization of the same investment. This may be the main reason that Microsoft's operating systems have become the overwhelming preference for businesses, that is, the practice of making a living.

There are many casual or recreational users of Apple® systems, but the vast majority of users who actual earn a living through the use of a computer, do so on a machine running one of Microsoft's operating systems. The largest estimate of all applications for all operating systems other than Microsoft® combined is less than 5% and for technical applications this less than 3%. It is estimated that almost 50% of all computers are running Windows-7® and that 10% are still running Windows-XP®.

Microsoft® has maintained a level of compatibility across multiple versions of its operating system, but this has not always been the case with business and scientific applications. There are many applications that will not run on Windows-7® or subsequent versions of the Microsoft® operating system. Many software developers are struggling to bring their applications out of the Windows-XP® era. This is readily evident in the food service and medical fields, where it is common to see ten-year-old desktop computers still running Windows-XP®.

While there may be other motivations (for example, keeping that stream of revenue coming in), the principle reason these applications are not compatible with Windows-7® and beyond is code development, that is, the way they were written. This is also why it has been so difficult to migrate some applications to the later operating systems, often requiring a complete re-write. In many cases, these applications have been around for so long that the original developers are no longer available to effect a migration.

This situation was entirely avoidable and would never have become such a problem if the developers of these applications had followed a few guidelines while writing the code in the first place. It is not only possible to write applications that are compatible with every version of the Windows® operating system, it much more efficient to do so. The same decisions and methods that lead to incompatibilities also result in poor performance and more bugs to fix. The purpose of the guidelines presented here is to avoid these problems and improve performance as well as compatibility.

Chapter 1. What's Up with Compatibility?

Since the introduction of Windows® Vista®, software developers have been inundated with the following questions:

Why won't this application install? It worked fine before.

Why is this such a problem? You should have seen this coming.

Why can't you just fix it? You did it the first time.

How difficult can it be? It's still Windows®.

In some sense the users are right. It did work fine before. The developers should have seen this coming. In many cases the same people did develop the application to begin with. It is still Windows®, but things have changed and decisions have consequences. Before laying out what to do and what not to do, it will be helpful to analyze why this has happened. If for no other reason, this should serve as motivation for following these guidelines to avoid this situation in the future.

Phantom Folders

One of the biggest causes of compatibility issues came with the introduction of phantom folders. These are folders that appear to be located in one place, but actually reside somewhere else entirely or may not be a folder at all. The most familiar example of a phantom folder is the *desktop*.

Most users think the *desktop* is a place. It isn't. It's a folder. They also think it's at the top of everything, because that's where Windows® Explorer® shows it to be. There are actually several folders that are combined to create what appears to be a single entity: the *desktop*. The combining process can obviously lead to problems, conflicts, and unintended consequences.

The desktop is not where you think it is,
nor is it a single folder.

The folders that are combined to produce the *desktop* reside under the individual user as well as the public or system storage areas. These areas are buried under a rat's nest of folders, which may be hidden or inaccessible, depending on the user account. As the *desktop* is a convenient location, users often drag things to it, which causes other problems that will be discussed subsequently.

The *Program Files* and *Program Data* folders are also phantoms in Vista® and subsequent versions of Windows®. These are buried even deeper than the desktop and are always hidden. These folders are where applications have traditionally been installed and this is the source of many compatibility issues. Most applications developed for Windows-XP® and before presumed necessary files would be in a particular location.

Problems arise when an application looks for a file in one location when it's logically somewhere else on the hard drive. The file appears to be in the right place when viewing the folders with Windows® Explorer®, but it's not really there. It's a phantom. Unless the software was developed with this in mind and the developer knew where to look for the file or used special function calls to open the file in the phantom location, the file won't be found and the application won't run.

Vista® and subsequent versions of the Windows® operating won't let you create a folder named Program Files *or* Program Data *in the logical location on the hard drive; so that's not a solution to the phantom folder problem.*

To complicate matters, these phantom folders are kept in different locations within the logical structure of the hard drive, depending on the version of Windows® as well as the type of user account. Phantom folders should never have been introduced in the first place, but they are here to stay, so don't put anything in them that you care to access.

It matters where files are actually *located within the logical structure, not where they* appear *to be located.*

Another compatibility issue that arises from the existence of phantom folders is the problem of combined file name and path length. The actual path to a phantom folder may begin with C:\Documents and Settings\Your Name\ Application Data\Microsoft\Office\Roaming, which adds 77 characters to the length. While it is possible to access files having path names longer than 255 characters, most software cannot handle this[1]. Even if you can trick older software into looking for files in these locations, this may result in array overruns.

Which Explorer?

There are two Microsoft® utilities called *Explorer®*: *Windows Explorer®* and *Internet Explorer®*. The former is a file management utility and the latter is a web browser. The two have little in common, but Microsoft® wants users to freely *explore* cyberspace without worrying about such details. Rather than enhancing the experience, this lack of distinction only causes confusion.

Files that physically reside on your computer or on other computers connected over a network are different from those that physically reside on a server in Malaysia. The format and content of such files is probably different and your access to them is definitely different. Pretending that this isn't the case and blurring the distinction may seem less complicated and may temporarily unburden users with details, butt this practice will return to byte you in the boot sector.

One thing these two *Explorers* have in common is that what you see may not be what you get. These two utilities show the location of objects that does

---

[1]Accessing files with very long path names is addressed in Appendix F.

not necessarily correspond to the physical or even logical location. The most egregious example of this is hyperlinks, which may say, "Click here to claim your free coupon," but may point to, "Install Trojan horse from Kazakhstan."[2]

Just because Windows Explorer® shows a file to be in a particular location doesn't mean that it's logically where it appears to be or that you can open it with the folder structure as displayed.

Access to files and associated resources is essential to the function of applications. The existence of phantom folders cannot be overlooked when developing applications.

Links vs. Files

Another important distinction that is foolishly blurred by Windows® Explorer® and often found on the desktop is that of links to files. By default Explorer® is set to hide file extensions. This option is set in *Control Panel* under *Folder Options*, as illustrated below:

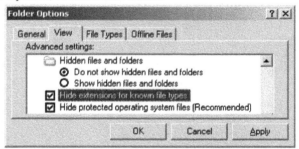

Users are often unaware of the distinction between files and links to files. When file extensions are hidden, a file named document1.doc.lnk, which is a link to the document, and not the document itself, may appear as document1.doc. Important files are often lost when users who are unaware of this distinction get a new computer. They copy the links from the desktop of the old computer to a thumb drive and then onto the desktop of the new computer, thinking they have copied the files. All they have copied are the links to the files. The files themselves–along with their content–are forever lost when the old computer is discarded.

OLE: Object Linking and Embedding

While it may be convenient to utilize someone else's software to operate on an object from inside yours, this is a foolish decision you will regret when it comes time to migrate your software to the next version of the operating system. OLE is a train wreck you should have considered before leaving the station.

---

[2]Why this dangerous behavior was ever created in the first place and why it hasn't been eliminated?

Some common examples include: using MSWord® to edit text from inside your patient scheduling software or using MSPaint® to modify an image from inside your inventory software.

If your software depends on someone else's–over which you have no control–continuing to work in the same way across versions of the operating system, you're headed off the cliff into Dead Code Gulch. Don't be surprised when you get there. If you depend on Microsoft® development tools, such as Visual BASIC® or Visual Studio®, the dependence of your application on object linking and embedding may be subtle.

As we will see in the section on *Common Controls*, this setup for failure is integral to Visual BASIC®. Many of the handy little objects that are readily available within Visual BASIC® and save so much time creating powerful applications are actually doors leading into an endless swamp, filled with the quicksand of incompatibility. What appears to be a simple little drop-down list, when activated, calls up MSAccess®, like a demonic legion from beyond the grave–and your application won't work without it.

Just say, NO to OLE!

Convenience is a poor trade for compatibility. There's never a good enough reason to use Visual BASIC® for anything you plan to invest in.

<u>Third-Party DLLs and other Black Boxes</u>

Another major cause of version incompatibility is the pervasive dependence on third-party objects, or *black boxes*. These objects are often DLLs. Some DLLs are part of the operating system. You must maintain compatibility with these, as they provide everything from opening a file to drawing a box or pushing a button. These are not the problem. Third-party DLLs are the problem.

I can only think of two reasons why a code developer would depend on a third-party DLL to provide an essential function within their application: 1) they don't know how to do it (ignorance) or 2) they don't want to do it (sloth).

In summary, the two most common causes of version incompatibility are: 1) phantom folders resulting in files not being where they appear to be and 2) dependence on objects over which you have no control. The solution to both problems is simply don't do it: 1) don't put anything in these folders and don't expect anything to be in them and 2) don't depend on something that someone else wrote that you don't have the source code for and don't understand how it works.

6

Chapter 2. The Basics of Windows® Programming

Windows® is a *message-based* operating system. This means that passing messages back and forth controls everything. Programs are called *applications*. Applications must have one or more message loops. Message loops are a body of code that receives and processes messages. Messages can come from or be passed to the operating system and can be sent to and received from other message loops in the current or other applications.

Some messages can be ignored, while others must not be. The latter are called *critical* messages. Windows® has certain *stock* objects, which provide their own procedure to process messages. In some cases you can substitute your own procedure for these built-in ones in order to achieve some level of customization, but this is very limited and can result in unintended consequences and even impact the function of other applications that are also running.

Message Processing

Messages contain a wide variety of information, including such things as: the user pushed a button or selected something from the menu, you need to redraw this object, what font and color do you want to use for this text, the window has been created, moved, resized, or closed, the user has moved or clicked the mouse, etc. There are hundreds of different messages. In order to understand message processing, it is essential to understand what Windows® calls the parent/child relationship. The operating system sends most messages to the parent, *not* the child, and *never* the grandparent or great-grandparent.

Consider the case of an application that is displaying an about box in which are several texts and an OK button. Windows® will send messages regarding the texts to the about box procedure as the parent, *not* your application, which would be the grandparent. In this example your application will *not* receive messages regarding the font, color, or content of the texts. If you need to process these messages for some reason, you must create a special procedure, which will have its own message loop.

If you don't provide such a custom procedure, everything in your about box will look like whatever Windows® is currently using as defaults for that type of object. Furthermore, you must create such a procedure for each and every object for which you want to exercise any level control over the appearance or function. Windows® lets you assign a unique identifier to each object and you can use the same procedure for several objects by checking the unique identifier and customizing the procedure for each object.

The Structure of a Windows® Program

Every Windows® application must have a certain structure and it must perform certain tasks in a specific order. You must first register any of your user-defined objects, which include your main program. You can register other objects later, but you must register them with Windows® *before* you can create them.

Each of these objects that you will be registering is called a CLASS.[3] Windows® classes can have, among other things, an icon, a cursor, or a bitmap. If you have to load these into memory, such as resources, you will have to load them before you register the class. This means that it is possible to fail to load something necessary to register the main application class so that the main application window can't be created. When this happens you will not be able use it to display an error message. In that case you must either abort the process without notifying the user visually (you could write an error message to a file) or you must use a stock object, such as a message box, to notify the user of the error.

Before you create a user-defined object (the first of which will probably be the main application window), you must already have a procedure ready to process all the messages that are sent to your application, including the WM_CREATE message. Failure to do so will result in the program terminating or crashing. You can ignore some messages, such as WM_SETCURSOR, or you can specifically change the cursor when you receive this message. You can also accept the default processing by passing the message to DefWindowProc(), which, in the case of the WM_SETCURSOR message will display the cursor assigned to the class when you registered it. If you are working with a dialog box and want the default processing, you *must* pass the message to DefDlgProc() instead of DefWindowProc(). Passing windows messages to DefDlgProc() dialog box messages to DefWindowProc() will probably result in your application crashing.

Once you have registered your application and created your main window, your procedure should enter a loop that simply calls GetMessage() and then DispatchMessage() until you receive the WM_NULL message, at which time you return from WinMain() and the application terminates. You can terminate an application prematurely by calling ExitProcess(). A call to exit() will result in the same thing.

Even keystrokes result in messages: when a key is pressed and also when it is released. The status of the shift, alt, and ctl keys come separately, so that if you want to combine these, you must process keystroke messages by calling TranslateMessage() between GetMessage() and DispatchMessage(). You can also define what are called accelerators, which is a list of messages to be associated with particular keystrokes, such as F1 for help and alt-F4 for exit. In this case you must call TranslateAccelerator() before TranslateMessage() to pull these out of the queue before they're interpreted as having their default meaning. This is what your main program should look like:

---

[3]Don't confuse these with what are called classes in C++. Windows® classes existed before Bjarne Stroustrup envisioned C++. Windows® applications do not require C++.

```
int WINAPI WinMain(HINSTANCE hInstance,HINSTANCE
   hPrev,char*CmdLine,int Show)
{
MSG msg;
HACCEL hAccel;
hInst=hInstance;  /* save this globally, as you'll need
   it later */
if((hAccel=LoadAccelerators(hInst, "ACCEL"))==NULL)
   Abort("can't load accelerators");
LoadImages();
RegisterClasses();
CreateWindows();
while(GetMessage(&msg,NULL,0,0))
   {
   if(!TranslateAccelerator(msg.hwnd, hAccel,&msg))
      {
      TranslateMessage(&msg);
      DispatchMessage(&msg);
      }
   }
return((int)msg.wParam);
}
```

Prototyping vs. Ambiguity

All C compilers will parse and store function definitions when they are first encountered. This is called auto-prototyping. You can explicitly prototype functions with declarations, but it is a far better practice to thoughtfully order your code and allow the compiler to handle this.

You should define each function before it is called. This is not always possible when one function calls another, which in turn calls the first, but these are rare exceptions. It can be tedious to reorder an existing code in this way, which is why you should get into the habit of writing code in this order to begin with. This practice also eliminates ambiguities.

Every object and structure should precede its first reference.

9

Chapter 3. Objects and Controls

Developing applications that include a GUI involves manipulating objects and controls. Objects are structures that contain information and controls are GUI elements that perform some function. It is essential to distinguish between objects and controls that are built into the Windows® operating system and those that are not.

Stock Objects

Windows® recognizes several types of objects, including: bitmaps (or images), icons (a special type of image), pens, brushes, fonts, timers, and cursors (also called mouse pointers). These are called *stock* objects. All of the controls (e.g., boxes, buttons, and lists) are drawn using these objects (i.e., pens, brushes, and bitmaps).

You cannot add objects to Windows®, although you can do things with your own custom objects using the existing controls and stock objects. There are functions to facilitate your bookkeeping for custom objects, including allocating memory, associating an icon, sending messages to your procedure, etc.; but this shouldn't be construed as Windows® recognizing your custom objects.

Many applications, such as those developed in Visual BASIC® (VB), make extensive use of objects and controls that are not part of the Windows® operating system. This practice is so ubiquitous that these objects and controls are often thought to be standard, but they are not. The stock objects include:

BITMAP	This is a graphical image or picture. The color depth of BITMAPs must be 1, 4, 8, or 24 bits. These color depths correspond to 2 (2^1), 16 (2^4), 256 (2^8), and 16 million (2^{24}) colors, respectively. The 1, 4, and 8 bit images must also have a PALETTE. The PALETTE contains 8-bit (i.e., 0-255) red, green, and blue components and the values are the index into the PALETTE. For 24-bit images the values are the actual red, green, and blue components. Windows® does not recognize other color schemes, such as cyan, magenta, and yellow or other color depths. Some displays use 15 bit images, in which case there are 5 bits (i.e., 0-31) for the red, green, and blue components. Some images use 16 bit images, in which case the green component gets 6 bits, as the human eye can distinguish more shades of green than either red or blue, but Windows® doesn't recognize either of these formats. There are also 32-bit images, where the extra 8 bits (1 byte) is called the alpha component, but Windows® doesn't know what to do with this extra byte and your display can't do anything with it either, so it's just a waste. Still, some displays use 32-bit images, because the display memory can be accessed more quickly in multiples

	of 4 bytes instead of 3. While the Microsoft® documentation may indicate that images can be compressed using RLE (run-length encoding, the simplest form of compression), don't even think about using this, as your application will probably crash if you do.
PALETTE	This is a list of 8-bit red, green, and blue components used in displaying an image. Windows® maintains a stock PALETTE containing either 16 or 256 colors, which you can change, although doing so changes the color of everything on the old 16 and 256 color displays.
ICON	This is as special type of BITMAP that also has a transparency mask. Icons can only have 16 or 256 colors and the size of icons must be a power of two (namely, 8x8, 16x16, 32x32, 64x64, or 128x128). The transparency mask is a 1-bit (B&W) bitmap that indicates where to paint and where not to on a pixel-by-pixel basis. You can specify an ICON for various stock controls, such as buttons, and for your entire application. Windows® has several stock icons, including: a red stop sign, green question mark, a yellow exclamation mark, a blue information mark, an up, down, left, and right arrowhead button, and the minimize, maximize, and close buttons. If you want Windows® to use a particular icon by default for your application, make it a resource and assign it an index of 100. [Resources will be discussed subsequently.]
CURSOR	This is a special type of BITMAP that is only a transparency mask, that is, a 1-bit (B&W) bitmap that tells where to paint and where not to on a pixel-by-pixel basis. You can tell Windows® what shape of cursor to display (e.g., cross-hairs, arrowhead, or I-beam) when the mouse is over some stock controls, such as buttons, and for your entire application. Windows® has several stock cursors, including: an hourglass, an arrowhead, crosshairs, and an I-beam. The little arrows that appear when you can drag or resize a box are also stock cursors.
PEN	Pens are used to draw lines and have a single color and width (not necessarily equal to 1). There are also special pens that will invert the color (i.e., black to white or yellow to blue) of whatever is beneath them. Every time you want to change the color or width, you must create a new pen. When you're through using a pen you should *destroy* it.

	(*Destroy* is what Windows® calls deleting an object and freeing the associated memory.) Windows® has several stock pens, including: black, white, and null, all 1-pixel wide. There are no stock light or dark gray pens, although there are stock light and dark gray brushes. You must select a pen into a device context before you can draw anything with it. [Device contexts will be discussed subsequently.] You can only have one pen selected into a device context at a time. If you want to draw something with multiple colors, you must select and deselect a separate pen for each color. If you want to draw the edge of something but not fill the interior, you must select the NULL brush, otherwise Windows® will paint the interior with whatever brush was already selected into the device context.
BRUSH	Brushes are used to paint things. Brushes don't have a width, but they do have a color and can be solid or have a user-defined pattern, such as a checkerboard or diamonds. There are also special brushes that will invert the color (i.e., black to white or yellow to blue) of whatever is beneath them. Every time you want to change any attribute you must create a new brush. When you're through using a brush you should *destroy* it. (*Destroy* is what Windows® calls deleting an object and freeing the associated memory.) Windows® has several stock brushes, including: black, white, light gray, dark gray, hollow, and null, all of which are solid. There is also a trick by which you can get a HANDLE to a brush that Windows® is currently using to paint the background of Windows® (usually white) the edge of Windows® (usually black), the caption (often blue), buttons (usually light gray), and shadows (usually dark gray). [Handles will be discussed subsequently.] You must select a brush into a device context before you can draw anything with it. [Device contexts will be discussed subsequently.] You can only have one brush selected into a device context at a time. If you want to draw something with multiple colors, you must select and deselect a separate brush for each color. If you want to paint inside but not the edge of something you must select the NULL pen, otherwise Windows® will draw the edge with whatever pen was previously selected into the device context.
HANDLE	A handle is a unique identifier that Windows® uses to refer

	to an object, such as a pen, brush, bitmap, button, etc. There is often memory associated with an object handle, but you can't just access that memory directly (which might be an image, for instance). There is a special process you must go through in order to get exclusive access to that memory: you must get, lock, and then release it. Many program crashes are a result of not properly following these steps.
RECTANGLE	This is just a rectangle, defined by the left, right, width, and height. Note that Windows® paints from left to right and top to bottom; whereas, most people think of a display from the bottom left corner upward. Also be aware that a rectangle does not include the bottom or right edges.
POINT	This is a single pixel.
POLYLINE	This is a line having two or more points. In order to draw a polyline you must have already selected a pen into the device context. [Device contexts will be discussed subsequently.]
POLYGON	This is a closed polygon having two or more points. In order to draw a polygon you must have already selected a pen and a brush into the device context. [Device contexts will be discussed subsequently.]
POLYPOLYGON	This is a group of polygons, which may be overlapping, so that some areas are drawn, while others are not. A poly-polygon would be used to draw objects like O, P, Q, and R, but wouldn't be necessary for S, T, or U. The characters in TrueType fonts are defined by poly-polygons. In order to draw a poly-polygon you must have already selected a pen and a brush into the device context. [Device contexts will be discussed subsequently.]
REGION	A region is a collection of other objects, such as rectangles and polygons. Regions are typically used to crop painting, to prevent painting outside a box or to prevent painting inside a box. Before you can use a region you must select it into a device context. [Device contexts will be discussed subsequently.]
DEVICE CONTEXT	A device context is an object you can paint into or copy from and is accessed via a handle. You cannot draw into anything but a device context. Specifically, you cannot draw into a bitmap, even if you create it yourself, at least

	not with any Windows® tool. Of course, you can do whatever you want with your own bitmaps, but you'll have to write the code to do this on a pixel-by-pixel basis yourself. You can paint a bitmap into a device context and you can select a bitmap into a device context, paint into that device context, deselect the bitmap, and then save it as a file, but you can't select a bitmap into the device context for the display, as attempting to do so will crash your application. You can only select a bitmap into a memory device context that is compatible with the display. You also can't copy one bitmap into another bitmap. You must first create two different memory device contexts, select one bitmap into each, then paint from one into the other, deselect the bitmaps, and destroy the memory device contexts. Printing anything in Windows® is a huge undertaking, as this requires creating and manipulating several different types of device contexts.
FONT	A font is a series of bitmaps, one for each character. In order to draw text you must have a font. There are only six stock fonts: ANSI_FIXED_FONT: device-independent fixed-pitch (monospace) system font, ANSI_VAR_FONT: device-independent variable-pitch (proportional space) system font, DEVICE_DEFAULT_FONT: device-dependent font, OEM_FIXED_FONT: original equipment manufacturer (OEM) dependent fixed-pitch (monospace) font, SYSTEM_FIXED_FONT: fixed-pitch (monospace) system font used in Windows® versions earlier than 3.0. This stock object is provided for compatibility with earlier versions of Windows®, SYSTEM_FONT: the system font. By default, Windows® uses the system font to draw menus, dialog box controls, and text. In Windows® versions 3.0 and later, the system font is a proportionally spaced font; earlier versions of Windows® used a monospace system font. Note that none of these are necessarily Times New Roman, Arial, Helvetica, Calibri, or anything else you may be accustomed to seeing. By default these are typically MS Sans Serif before Windows-7® and Calibri after. You can change these, but they're not the same from one system to another and you shouldn't expect them to be. There is also no such thing as italic and/or bold, let alone Greek, subscript, or superscript. These stock fonts also do not include any of the following characters: ®¢£¥§¼½¾°23±®. If you want to display such

	things you must create a font, typically from one of the TrueType font files you have registered on your system. Note that italic, bold, and bold italic are three separate fonts. Each point size is also a separate font. The only thing you can change about a font once you've created it is the color of the foreground and background. Once you're through using a font you should *destroy* it. (*Destroy* is what Windows® calls deleting an object and freeing the associated memory.) You must also select a font into a device context before you can draw with it. You can only select one font into a device context at a time, so that if you want to display a text with italic or bold words, you must select and deselect each of these fonts as you draw each line of text, each word or character if you want them to have a different appearance.

In addition to these objects, Windows® has what are called controls. Controls include such things as boxes and buttons. There are only two types of objects: stock and custom. Stock objects are provided by the operating system at the most basic level, apart from any add-ons or service packs, and come with only a basic level of functionality.

You can customize the appearance and behavior of some stock objects, but this is limited. When you are customizing a stock object, such as a button, Windows® refers to this control as being OWNER-DRAWN, which means literally that: you must do *everything* yourself, as Windows® doesn't draw any part of it. Custom objects are user-created and you are responsible for *everything* about their appearance and function.

You create custom objects by combining the features of one or more of the stock objects and drawing primitives (e.g., pens, brushes, and bitmaps). Even if you are using a custom object that has been provided by an add-on, such as an OCX or DLL, whoever wrote that add-on has created that custom object by combining the features of one or more of the stock objects and drawing primitives; *because there is no other way to do anything in Windows®.*

<u>Stock Controls</u>

In spite of the many things you are accustomed to seeing in Windows® applications, there are only seven stock objects, which are called *Controls*:

BUTTON	This can be a pushbutton, radio button, or check box. Anything else *must* be owner-drawn.
COMBOBOX	This is commonly called a drop-down list and has surprisingly little built-in functionality. *You* must provide most of the functionality you are accustomed to seeing. This control *does not,* for instance, come with a list of folders and files for you to

	choose from, or little icons, or anything else you might be accustomed to seeing.
EDIT	This is a text box that you can type into and is black text on a white background. You can change the color, but that takes some clever message processing. The stock edit control has surprisingly little functionality, although you can use ctl-C to copy and ctl-V to paste inside a stock EDIT control.
LISTBOX	This is a text box with optional horizontal and vertical scrollbars. This control *does not provide* word wrapping or what you're accustomed to thinking of as tabs, although it can provide tabs that are more like column separators. You can control the font, the color of the text, and the color of the background, but it will be the same for every word in line of text. *If you want anything else, you will have to draw the entire thing yourself!*
MDICLIENT	This is a frame that handles child windows that you're accustomed to seeing which can be cascaded or tiled vertically or tiled horizontally. This is only the frame. The MDICLIEN *doesn't provide any other functionality* for the child windows.
SCROLLBAR	This is only the track and the button and can be either vertical or horizontal. If you're using both, then you'll have two of these. This control only draws the track and the button, but *it doesn't do anything with it!* In other words, when you move a scrollbar button, Windows® doesn't scroll your window for you. Windows® merely informs you that the button has been moved. You have to do whatever it takes to scroll the window. The only thing Windows® will scroll for you is a LISTBOX.
STATIC	This control can contain text, which can be left, right, or centered. This control *does not provide* what is commonly called full justification, that is, both left and right alignment, but it can provide word wrapping. You can add a horizontal or vertical scrollbar to a STATIC control, but these won't do anything and you can't make Windows move the text back and forth or up and down with the scrollbars. In order to do that you would have to make this an OWNERDRAW STATIC control, in which case you would have to actually draw the text as well as everything else, including the scrollbars and frame. This control can also contain an ICON or BITMAP (which are different: icons are limited in size and color depth an have a transparency mask; whereas, bitmaps can have a wide range of color depths and have no transparency mask).

	You can specify the icon at the time you create a STATIC control, but you must link a bitmap *after* the control has already been created and you are limited as to what types of bitmaps will be drawn automatically. You must provide custom code in order to actually paint any other kind of bitmap.

That's it. *There are no other stock controls!* There are, however, a few *extended* controls. Before defining the extended controls we should define what Windows® calls a DIALOG object or a dialog box. A dialog box is simply a popup window that contains one or more of these stock controls, such as text and a pushbutton.

Windows provides one somewhat customizable dialog object by calling MessageBox(). As part of this call you can specify the caption, some text, one of the stock icons (e.g., the stop sign, exclamation point, or question mark) and some combination of buttons, including: OK, Yes, No, and Cancel. If you've done anything with Windows you've seen a lot of things displayed by calling MessageBox().

Extended Controls

There are fourteen Windows *extended* controls. These are called *Common Controls* and are defined in the include file commctrl.h. The functionality is provided in commctrl.dll for 16-bit programs and comctl32.dll for 32- and 64-bit programs, both of which are part of the basic Windows operating system. The Common Controls are:

ANIMATE	This control displays a series of bitmaps in a box at a specified rate. The bitmaps must be stored in a certain order and format and cannot be compressed. You could do the same thing with a STATIC control and a timer loop.
DRAGLIST	This control is like a combination of a LISTBOX with tabbed headers. This control will sort the list by columns when you click on the tabs at the top.
HEADER	This control is similar to the TOOLBAR control except that the buttons have text instead of pictures and they don't have to be square or sized in powers of two.
HOTKEY	This control doesn't draw anything. It only facilitates defining hot keys and associated messages. This functionality is usually accomplished with a list of accelerators, which will be described subsequently.
IMAGELIST	This control draws a series of images much like the TOOLBAR, but without the buttons.

LISTVIEW	This control draws something like a LISTBOX with little icons on the left. It also doesn't do anything besides notify you that something has been selected. Using this extended control is better than drawing the entire thing yourself, but you will be quite surprised just how complicated it is to generate something like a file and folder selection list.
MENUHELP	This control facilitates the display of popup text, such as help information. This functionality is usually accomplished by providing a help file or displaying an about box.
PROGRESS	This control doesn't do anything besides draw the bar and frame. You must update its position to indicate whatever progress is going on elsewhere.
STATUSBAR	This is just a gray frame that you can write black text into. The frame appears sunken and is often used at the bottom of an application window. You could do the same thing with an OWNERDRAW STATIC control.
TABCONTROL	This control draws the little tabs that are at the bottom of Excel or often found in applications where objects are grouped and only one group is displayed at a time. This control doesn't do anything but draw the tabs and notify you when the user clicks on a tab. This control *does not have any* impact on what's displayed beneath or above the tabs and *does not show or hide anything* else. *You must do all that yourself!*
TOOLBAR	This control draws the familiar bar across the top of many applications that has little icon buttons, such as open, close, print, copy, paste, etc. This control *doesn't do anything* besides drawing the buttons and notifying you when a button has been pushed. All the icons must be the same size and contained in a single bitmap positioned next to each other in a single row. Furthermore, you are limited as to the color depth (16 or 256 colors) and size of the icons (must be a power of two: 8x8, 16x16, 32x32, 64x64, or 128x128).
TRACKBAR	This control works like a SCROLLBAR except with a pointer on a line rather than a button on a track, but otherwise works the same and *doesn't do anything* other than draw itself and notify you when it's moved.
TREEVIEW	This control draws what you're accustomed to seeing as folders, subfolders, and files when you're getting ready to

	open or save a file. *This control isn't filled for you and doesn't do anything but notify you when the user makes as selection. You must do everything else!* You can change the little icons that typically look like a little yellow open or closed folder.
UPDOWN	This control draws two buttons having opposing arrows, either up/down or left/right. This control *doesn't do anything* besides drawing the buttons and notifying you when one has been pushed.

In order to use any of these extended controls, you must specifically load the appropriate DLL by calling the function InitCommonControls(). If the call is unsuccessful, and Windows doesn't inform you one way or the other, your controls simply won't display and your application may crash. The same thing happens if you forget to call this function.

Common Dialogs

Windows® also has eight common dialogs, which you have seen on many occasions. These are:

Color	Displays available colors as well as controls that allow the user to define custom colors.
Font	Displays lists of fonts and point sizes that correspond to available fonts. After the user selects a font, the dialog box displays sample text rendered with that font.
Open	Displays a list of filenames matching any specified extensions, directories, and drives. By selecting one of the listed filenames, the user indicates the file an application should open.
Save As	Displays a list of filenames matching any specified extensions, directories, and drives. By selecting one of the listed filenames, the user indicates the file an application should save.
Print	Displays information about the installed printer and its configuration. By altering and selecting controls in this dialog box, the user specifies how output should be printed and starts the printing process. *Note: this doesn't print anything! It only facilitates the start of the process. You must do everything else.*
Print Setup	Displays the current printer configuration and provides options for setting the paper orientation, size, and source (when the printer driver supports these options). The Print Setup dialog box can be called directly, or it can be opened from within the Print dialog box. *Note: this doesn't print anything!*

Find	Displays an edit control in which the user can type a string for an application to search. The user can specify which direction to search, whether the application should match the case of the specified string, and whether the string to match is an entire word. *Note: this doesn't actually find anything!*
Replace	Displays two edit controls in which the user can type strings. The first string identifies a word or value that the application should replace, and the second string identifies the replacement word or value. *Note: this doesn't actually find or replace anything!*

These common dialogs are very helpful in building most any Windows® application. If you need to select a folder rather than a file, use the undocumented function SHBrowseForFolder(), which is defined in shlobj.h. The file selection dialog box on recent versions of Windows® also provides a preview of the images contained in bitmap files, if the iconic view option is selected. As this feature only works for Windows®-compatible bitmaps, many applications provide their own file open and save dialogs, which provide previews of a wider range of content.

Resources

Windows® programs make much use of what are called *Resources*. Resources function in a manner similar to a data statement in that they are pre-compiled static blocks of data. Two differences are that resources can be created for objects that the compiler can't read and they are appended to the executable file, rather than being embedded along with the compiled code. There is a separate resource compiler. The linker combines the .OBJ file from the C compiler with the .RES file from the resource compiler and creates the .EXE file. Windows® resources include:

BITMAP	These must be a .BMP file and must have 1, 4, 8, or 24-bit color depth and must not be compressed.
CURSOR	These must be a .CUR file.
DIALOG	These are static dialog boxes and are specified in the .RC file, which is plain text. You can also create dynamic dialog boxes in memory.
FONT	These must be a .FON or .TTY file.
KEYBOARD ACCELERATOR	This is a list of messages to associate with various keystrokes and is defined in the .RC file, which is plain text.
ICON	These must be a .ICO file. By default Windows® will use the first one it finds if you don't give it a number of 100 or

	manually associated it with your application class.
MENU	These are specified in the .RC file, which is plain text.
STRING TABLE	These are Unicode strings.
RCBINARY	This data type is copied as-is. This is the type you would use for a GIF or JPG. You would have to decompress either one of these yourself and convert them to a BITMAP before you could paint them, as *Windows®* *does not recognize either one of these image formats.*

Accelerators, cursors, dialogs, fonts, icons, and menu resources are easily accessed, as there is a function to fetch each one, LoadAccelerators(), LoadCursor(), etc. Bitmaps and binary resources are a little more complicated. While there is a function LoadBitmap(), it doesn't exactly return what you need if you intend to do anything with the bitmap. The resource compiler strips the file header off a bitmap and adds another useless header before storing it as a resource.

If you want to use a bitmap for anything, you will need to get past that: First you must actually get the resource into memory where you can access it, which is the same process required for loading a binary resource. There are three steps you must take, called find, load, and lock. If you skip any one of these or if any step fails your program will crash. This is how you load a resource and a bitmap:

```
void*GetResource(char*rname,char*type)
{
void*rLock;
HGLOBAL rLoad;
HRSRC rFind;
if((rFind=FindResource(hInst,rname,type))==NULL)
  return(NULL);
if((rLoad=LoadResource(hInst,rFind))==NULL)
  return(NULL);
if((rLock=LockResource(rLoad))==NULL)
  return(NULL);
return(rLock);
}


BITMAPINFOHEADER*LoadBitmapResource(char*rname)
{
return((BITMAPINFOHEADER*)
  ((BYTE*)GetResource(rname,RT_BITMAP)));
}
```

This is a typical resource file:

```
#include "windows.h"

MYICON ICON "MYICON.ICO"
```

```
ABOUT BITMAP "ABOUT.BMP"
EXIT BITMAP "EXIT.BMP"
HELP BITMAP "HELP.BMP"

IMAGE1 RT_RCDATA "IMAGE1.GIF"
IMAGE2 RT_RCDATA "IMAGE2.GIF"
IMAGE3 RT_RCDATA "IMAGE3.JPG"

MY_MENU MENU
  BEGIN
    POPUP "&File"
    BEGIN
      MENUITEM "E&xit", MENU_EXIT
    END
    POPUP "&Help"
    BEGIN
      MENUITEM "&About...", MENU_ABOUT
    END
  END

ABOUT DIALOG 22, 17, 158, 61
  STYLE DS_MODALFRAME | WS_CAPTION | WS_SYSMENU |
  WS_OVERLAPPED
  CAPTION "About this Program"
  FONT 8, "System"
  BEGIN
    LTEXT "Company", ID_COMPANY, 6,2,100,8, SS_LEFT
    LTEXT "Description", ID_DESCRIPTION, 6,11,100,8,
    SS_LEFT
    LTEXT "Version", ID_VERSION, 6,20,137,8, SS_LEFT
    LTEXT "Copyright", ID_COPYRIGHT, 6,29,137,8, SS_LEFT
    CONTROL "", 0, "Static", SS_BLACKRECT, 5,43,138,1
    LTEXT "Trademarks", ID_TRADEMARKS, 6,47,136,10,
    SS_LEFT
    DEFPUSHBUTTON "OK", IDOK, 121,2,32,14, WS_GROUP
  END

MY_ACCEL ACCELERATORS
  BEGIN
    VK_F4, MENU_EXIT, VIRTKEY, ALT
  END
```

Using Bitmaps

If you want to paint a bitmap into a static control (i.e., a box) or onto a button, what you'll need is a pointer to the bitmap info header, which is what the function above returns. The palette, if there is one, follows directly after the header and the image data follows directly after the palette. This is how you paint a bitmap:

```
void PaintBitmap(HDC
   hDC,RECT*rc,BITMAPINFOHEADER*bHead,int stretch)
{
int colors,h,H,l,t,w,W;
BYTE*bImage;
l=rc->left;
t=rc->top;
w=rc->right-rc->left;
h=rc->bottom-rc->top;
W=bHead->biWidth;
H=bHead->biHeight;
if(bHead->biBitCount==24)
   colors=0;
else
   {
   colors=bHead->biClrUsed;
   if(colors==0)
      colors=1<<bHead->biBitCount;
   }
bImage=((BYTE*)bHead)+sizeof(BITMAPINFOHEADER)
   +colors*sizeof(DWORD);
if(stretch)
   StretchDIBits(hDC,l,t,w,h,0,0,W,H,bImage,
   (BITMAPINFO*)bHead,
      DIB_RGB_COLORS,SRCCOPY);
else if(w*abs(H)<abs(W)*h)
   StretchDIBits(hDC,l,t+(h-
   w*abs(H)/abs(W))/2,w,w*abs(H)/abs(W),
      0,0,W,H,bImage,
   (BITMAPINFO*)bHead,DIB_RGB_COLORS,SRCCOPY);
else
   StretchDIBits(hDC,l+(w-
   h*abs(W)/abs(H))/2,t,h*abs(W)/abs(H),h,
      0,0,W,H,bImage,
   (BITMAPINFO*)bHead,DIB_RGB_COLORS,SRCCOPY);
}
```

Device Contexts

Windows® API function calls don't do anything with bitmaps (i.e., images) directly. All of the related structures and functions are defined in wingdi.h. These functions work with *handles* to bitmaps, not *pointers* to bitmaps. If you implement your own code, you will need *pointers*, not *handles*. The former are obtained from the latter with a call to GetObject(). If you ever intend to use a bitmap with an API call, you must use an API call to create that bitmap, rather than using malloc() and filling it yourself. CreateDIBSection() is used to create anything other than a B&W bitmap.

There are many useful and powerful API functions, but these only work with device contexts. If you want to do something with a bitmap, you must first

24

select it into a device context. You can only select one bitmap into a device context at a time, so that if you want to copy something from one bitmap to another, you must have two separate device contexts and select one bitmap into each. Don't forget to deselect a bitmap when you're finished with it and before you lose or destroy the device context.

There is no limit to the number of device contexts, but you should either keep track of them and reuse them or destroy them when you no longer need them. It does take some time to create a device context, so if you plan to use a device context many times, it is best to create and reuse the same one over again. Most of the time when you are performing operations with bitmaps you will be using a memory device context created with a call to the API function CreateCompatibleDC().

Simple Dialog Boxes

Simple dialog boxes are an important part of any Windows® application. Simple dialog boxes have text and buttons, but *not* EDIT controls. Making edit controls function properly is a good bit more complicated and will be covered subsequently. The most common type of simple dialog box is the about box. A typical about box dialog was provided above in the example resource file. Putting this in the resource file is only the first step in actually implementing an about box. The next step is loading it when the user selects this from the menu. Put the following in your main procedure:

```
if(wMsg==WM_COMMAND&&LOWORD(wParam)==MENU_ABOUT)
{
DialogBox(hInst,"ABOUT",hMain, (DLGPROC)AboutProc);
return(FALSE);
}
```

This will load the dialog resource and route all messages to AboutProc() until you push the OK button. This is what AboutProc() should look like:

```
LRESULT WINAPI AboutProc(HWND hWnd,DWORD wMsg,DWORD
   wParam,
   LPARAM lParam)
{
if(wMsg==WM_COMMAND)
  {
  if(HIWORD(wParam)==BN_CLICKED
|| HIWORD(wParam)==BN_DOUBLECLICKED)
  if(LOWORD(wParam)==IDOK)
     return(EndDialog(hWnd,LOWORD(wParam)));
  return(FALSE);
  }
if(wMsg==WM_CTLCOLORDLG)
  return((DWORD)GetStockObject(LTGRAY_BRUSH));
if(wMsg==WM_CTLCOLORSTATIC)
  {
  SetBkMode((HDC)wParam,TRANSPARENT);
```

```
      SetTextColor((HDC)wParam,BLACK);  /* your text color
*/
      SelectObject((HDC)wParam,hYourFont);/* put your font
*/
      return((DWORD)GetStockObject(LTGRAY_BRUSH));
      }
   if(wMsg==WM_INITDIALOG)
      {
      int high,left,top,wide;
      RECT wR;
```
GetWindowRect(hWnd,&wR);
```
      wide=wR.right-wR.left;
      high=wR.bottom-wR.top;
      left=(GetSystemMetrics(SM_CXSCREEN)-wide)/2;
      top=(GetSystemMetrics(SM_CYSCREEN)-high)/2;
      MoveWindow(hWnd,left,top,wide,high,TRUE);
      SetWindowText(hWnd,"your caption here");
      SetDlgItemText(hWnd,ID_COMPANY,"your company here");
      SetDlgItemText(hWnd,ID_DESCRIPTION,"your description
      here");
      SetDlgItemText(hWnd,ID_VERSION,"your version here");
      SetDlgItemText(hWnd,ID_COPYRIGHT,"your copyright");
      SetDlgItemText(hWnd,ID_TRADEMARKS,"your
      trademarks");
      return(TRUE);
      }
   return(FALSE);
   }
```

This will center the about box on the screen and fill it with your text in the color and font you want. Of course, you only get one font and one color, unless you check the handle passed with the `WM_CTLCOLORSTATIC message and compare` it to each one of the IDs to see which one it is and then select that font, which you must have already created, as in the following example (remember, the message is being sent to the parent, not the control itself):

```
   if((HWND)lParam==GetDlgItem(hWnd,ID_COMPANY))
      SelectObject((HDC)wParam,hCompanyFont);
   else if((HWND)lParam==GetDlgItem(hWnd,ID_DESCRIPTION))
      SelectObject((HDC)wParam,hDescriptionFont);
   etc.
```

Disabling the Close [X] Box

More often than not, you want the user to make some sort of decision, such as actually pushing the Yes, No, or Cancel buttons or actually entering a number into an EDIT control in a dialog box. If you have a caption, you get a close [X] button, whether you want it or not. Fortunately, you can make it so that the user can't push it, should you want to do so, simply insert this line of code where you process the **WM_INITDIALOG**:

26

```
EnableMenuItem(GetSystemMenu(hWnd,FALSE),
    SC_CLOSE,MF_GRAYED);
```

Combo Boxes or Drop Down Selections

There are several things about the **COMBOBOX** (or drop down selection) controls that just don't work properly, perhaps the most annoying of which is that the user can type into it when you only want them to select one of a list of things you've provided. You keep the user from typing in an invalid selection by disabling this function at the time of initialization, as illustrated in the following code sample:

```
if(wMsg==WM_INITDIALOG)
{
dialog1.edit1=GetWindow(dialog1.combo1, GW_CHILD);
SendMessage(dialog1.edit1,EM_SETREADONLY, TRUE,0);
```

Controlling the color is also complicated. This is all because, in spite of it's being a **COMBOBOX**, it sends control messages, including color notifications, to the parent as having come from a STATIC, EDIT, and/or LISTBOX object, because this control is actually built up from these other controls. This means that what you think is the parent window procedure receiving the message is actually the *grand*parent, that is, the edit, static, and listbox controls are children of the combo box, which is a child of the window receiving the notifications; and *only* the parent window receives notifications, *not* the *grand*parent. You may want the combo box items to have black text on a white background, but the other static texts to have black text on a light gray background. The following section of code shows how to make these objects display in the proper colors:

```
if(wMsg==WM_CTLCOLOREDIT||
    wMsg==WM_CTLCOLORLISTBOX||
    (wMsg==WM_CTLCOLORSTATIC&&
    ((HWND)lParam==dialog1.combo1||
    (HWND)lParam==dialog1.edit1)))
{

SelectObject((HDC)wParam,GetStockObject(ANSI_VAR_FONT
));
SetBkMode((HDC)wParam,TRANSPARENT);
SetTextColor((HDC)wParam,BLACK);
return((LRESULT)GetStockObject(WHITE_BRUSH));
}
if(wMsg==WM_CTLCOLORSTATIC)
{
SelectObject((HDC)wParam,
    GetStockObject(ANSI_VAR_FONT));
SetBkMode((HDC)wParam,TRANSPARENT);
SetTextColor((HDC)wParam,BLACK);
return((LRESULT)GetStockObject(LTGRAY_BRUSH));
```

}

If the message is coming from the static control, that is the child of the combo box, it will be intercepted by the first if(), otherwise it will be intercepted by the second. In order to intercept these messages and properly process them, you must get and save the handle of these controls; otherwise you can't distinguish them from the other controls of the same type. You must get the handles when the dialog box is initialized and save them in a global variable, in this example dialog1.combo1 and dialog1.edit1, as in the following sample code:

```
if(wMsg==WM_INITDIALOG)
{
dialog1.combo1=GetDlgItem(hWnd,ID_COMBO1);
dialog1.edit1=GetWindow(dialog1.combo1, GW_CHILD);
```

You must also fill the listbox child of the combo box at the time of initialization, because the resource compiler has no provision for preloading it. The following sample code will accomplish this:

```
if(wMsg==WM_INITDIALOG)
{
SendDlgItemMessage(hWnd,ID_COMBO1,
  CB_ADDSTRING,0,(LPARAM)"apples");
SendDlgItemMessage(hWnd,ID_COMBO1,
  CB_ADDSTRING,0,(LPARAM)"oranges");
SendDlgItemMessage(hWnd,ID_COMBO1,
  CB_ADDSTRING,0,(LPARAM)"peaches");
SendDlgItemMessage(hWnd,ID_COMBO1,
  CB_ADDSTRING,0,(LPARAM)"pears");
```

The Group Box

A group box is actually a type of button, which accepts no input and looks something like the following:

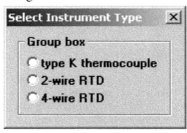

The default behavior of the group box is somewhat problematic and can be confusing. If you create the group box first and then add the three radio buttons, all as children of the larger dialog box, you will not be able to see or select the three radio buttons; because they will be beneath and obscured by the group box. If you create the three radio buttons before you create the group box, all as

28

children of the larger dialog box, the three radio buttons won't work as a group, allowing you to select only one of the three and cycling through the selections.

In order for the three radio buttons to work correctly, you must first create the group box as a child of the larger dialog box, and then create the three radio buttons as children of the group box. Of course, this also means that the messages you might like for the dialog to receive will only be sent to the group box, which is actually a type of button, and not the dialog.

If you create them in this order, the three radio buttons will work properly, but you won't always know which one of the radio buttons the user has selected, nor will you be able to properly update other items that may depend on which type of instrument is selected. This is because the notification messages from the radio buttons are sent to their parent, the group box, not the *grand*parent, the dialog box.

Furthermore, even if you report every message received by your application, you'll never see these notifications, because they are what's called *non-queued* (or internal) messages, as opposed to *queued* (or external) messages. These messages are sent directly to the group box. So you can't fix this undesired behavior with enhanced message processing alone.

As a stock control, group boxes have their own message handling procedure. If you need to intercept these messages you will have to hook into Windows®' procedure and pick them off as they arrive, being very careful to not interfere with any of the messages. This is called *subclassing*:

> *When an application creates a window, the operating system allocates a block of memory for storing information specific to the window, including the address of the window procedure that processes messages for the window. When Windows® needs to pass a message to the window, it searches the window-specific information for the address of the window procedure and passes the message to that procedure.*

> *Subclassing is a technique that allows an application to intercept and process messages sent or posted to a particular window before the window has a chance to process them. By subclassing a window, an application can augment, modify, or monitor the behavior of the window. Although it is not recommended an application can subclass any window, including those belonging to a system global class, such as an edit control or a list box. For example, an application could subclass an edit control to prevent the control from accepting certain characters. For an explanation of the risks involved, see the following section.*

An application subclasses a window by replacing the address of the window's original window procedure with the address of a new window procedure, called the subclass procedure. Thereafter, the subclass procedure receives any messages sent or posted to the window.

The subclass procedure can take three actions upon receiving a message: it can pass the message to the original window procedure, modify the message and pass it to the original window procedure, or process the message and not pass it to the original window procedure. If the subclass procedure processes a message, it can do so before, after, or both before and after it passes the message to the original window procedure.

This same problem occurs with a combo box that might look something like the following:

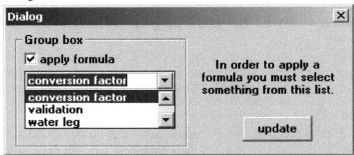

If you don't subclass or replace the stock class you will not be notified when the user changes the selection until after they push the update button and close the dialog, which would be too late to check for validity or conflicts or update other choices. If you don't un-subclass the procedure before you exit, if, for instance, your program crashes, you risk locking-up your application or crashing Windows® altogether.

An additional complication with the COMBOBOX control arises from its consisting of several other controls: an EDIT or STATIC box, the drop-down BUTTON, and the drop-down LISTBOX. The EDIT or STATIC box displays the current selection. If the user can type into the selection, then an EDIT control is used. If the user can't type into the selection, then a STATIC control is used.

The BUTTON activates the drop-down and displays the LISTBOX, which is otherwise hidden. These three controls are all children of the COMBOBOX and communicate with it using *non-queued* messages, which you won't see unless you subclass the COMBOBOX.

The EDIT Control

The default behavior of EDIT controls is so problematic that it requires special attention. EDIT controls and buttons can be logically grouped together when they are all children of a dialog box or main window. These groups have nothing to do with a GROUP box. Consider the following example dialog box:

Width, Height, and Resolution STATIC controls and are children of the Image Dimensions GROUP box. The 1024, 64, and 72 are EDIT controls and are also children of the GROUP box. The Pixels and Pixels/inch are COMBOBOX controls and children of the GROUP box. The GROUP box, OK, Cancel, and Help buttons are children of the New Image DIALOG box.

If the 1024, 64, and 72 EDIT controls have the style WS_GROUP, when you press the tab key, the focus (blue highlight) will move from one to the next. Pressing the shift tab key will move from one control to the next in the opposite order. This behavior can also be manifested in the OK, Cancel, and Help buttons. When a button is selected (the OK button is currently selected and has a dark border) and you press the spacebar, Windows® will interpret this as you pressing that button.

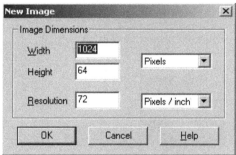

The tab key isn't the problem with the EDIT control. The Enter key is the problem. You are told to, "Enter a number in the box." How do you accomplish this? You type something and then press the Enter key. No one tells you to, "Tab a number in the box." If you type "800" in the box that currently contains "1024" and press the Enter key, Windows® will push the OK key for you–whether you wanted it to or not. If you had pressed the tab key instead, focus would drop to the 64 EDIT control.

Getting the EDIT controls in this DIALOG to work properly is surprisingly difficult. This particular one came from Paint Shop and doesn't work properly. The way this dialog is supposed to behave is:

1) You type a number in the 1024 box and press Enter.

2) Focus drops down to the 64 box, you type something, and press Enter.

3) Focus drops down to the 72 box, you type something, and press Enter.

4) Focus shifts to the Pixels drop-down.

As mentioned previously, important messages from the EDIT controls will be sent *internally* to the GROUP box and you will never see them. It is possible; however, to make this dialog work correctly, by following these steps:

1) Disable the parent process to stop messages from going to its loop.

2) Launch a modeless dialog rather than a modal dialog. If you launch a modal dialog Windows® internal loop will process the messages.

3) Begin a message loop. Look for the Enter key message and replace it with a Tab key message.

4) Kill the modeless dialog when a button is pressed.

5) Enable the parent process so that it will begin receiving messages again.

This logic is illustrated in the following code snippet:

```
EnableWindow(hParent,FALSE);
CreateDialog(hInst,Rname,hMain,Proc);
while(GetMessage(&wMsg,NULL,0,0))
{
if(wMsg.message==WM_KEYDOWN)
  if(wMsg.wParam==VK_RETURN)
    wMsg.wParam=VK_TAB;
if(!TranslateMessage(&wMsg))
  DispatchMessage(&wMsg);
}
EnableWindow(hParent,TRUE);
```

Chapter 4. The Secret to Version-Independence

If it isn't listed in the preceding chapter on *Objects and Controls,* don't use it. It's not part of Windows®. If it's some object that's only been added to a recent version of Windows®, don't use it. Follow the principle of the least common denominator: use only those objects and controls that have always been part of Windows®. You cannot depend on anything else to function in the same way or to even be available in subsequent versions of the operating system.

If you must have it, then build it from the objects and controls previously listed. Anything necessary for developing a GUI can be built from these foundational objects and controls. If you have written code that is dependent on a third-party library for some other functionality, rest assured that whoever wrote that library built its functionality from these objects and controls.

In order to achieve version-independence, you *must* eliminate all third-party libraries from your build. You must either acquire the source code–along with the expertise to modify and maintain it–or you must develop the code yourself. This is also a quality control gap the size of the Grand Canyon.

As long as you're relying on a third party–over whom you have no control–you cannot achieve version-independence.

You may be using third party objects and controls without being aware of it. When your code is written in C this is easy to determine from the *include*.h and *link*.lib files required to build the application. If any of these files didn't come with the Microsoft® C compiler, then by definition they're third party and you shouldn't be using them.[4]

The secret to version-independence is not complicated: just don't use anything that hasn't always been part of Windows® and don't even think about using the *Program Files* or *Program Data* folders. The complicated part is how to achieve the functionality you want with the objects and controls you have to work with. That is the subject of the rest of this book. Accomplishing this isn't obvious or easy, but it is possible, as illustrated previously on how to make EDIT controls work properly.

---

[4]Everything you need to compile and link programs written in C for the Windows® operating system can be obtained without cost from Microsoft®, as described in Appendix A.

Chapter 5. Working with BUTTONs

If you want to create a row of buttons, as illustrated below:

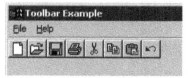

The easiest way to do this is with the TOOLBAR extended control as described previously. First, you will need a bitmap that looks like this:

Put this bitmap, along with a list of strings to be used as tool tips when the cursor hovers over each button, in a resource file, as in the following example:

```
ID_BITMAP BITMAP "TOOLBAR.BMP"
STRINGTABLE
  BEGIN
    ID_NEW   "Creates a new document"
    ID_OPEN  "Opens an existing document"
    ID_SAVE  "Saves the active document"
    ID_PRINT "Prints the active document"
    ID_CUT   "Cuts the selection and puts it on the
    clipboard"
    ID_COPY  "Copies the selection and puts it on the
    clipboard"
    ID_UNDO  "Reverses the last action"
    ID_PASTE "Inserts the clipboard contents at the
    insertion point"
    ID_UNDO  "Reverses the last action"
  END
```

Create a table that will associate each button with a command ID, as in:

```
TBBUTTON tbButton[]={
  {0,ID_NEW  ,TBSTATE_ENABLED,TBSTYLE_BUTTON,0,0},
  {1,ID_OPEN ,TBSTATE_ENABLED,TBSTYLE_BUTTON,0,0},
  {2,ID_SAVE ,TBSTATE_ENABLED,TBSTYLE_BUTTON,0,0},
  {3,ID_PRINT,TBSTATE_ENABLED,TBSTYLE_BUTTON,0,0},
  {4,ID_CUT  ,TBSTATE_ENABLED,TBSTYLE_BUTTON,0,0},
  {5,ID_COPY ,TBSTATE_ENABLED,TBSTYLE_BUTTON,0,0},
  {6,ID_PASTE,TBSTATE_ENABLED,TBSTYLE_BUTTON,0,0},
  {7,ID_UNDO ,TBSTATE_ENABLED,TBSTYLE_BUTTON,0,0}};
```

Call InitCommonControls(), register classes, create the main window, and then create the toolbar, as in:

```
hTool=CreateToolbarEx(hMain,WS_CHILD|WS_VISIBLE|
  TBSTYLE_TOOLTIPS,ID_TOOLBAR,sizeof(tbButton)/
  sizeof(tbButton[0]),hInst,ID_BITMAP,tbButton,
  sizeof(tbButton)/sizeof(TBBUTTON),16,16,16,16,
  sizeof(TBBUTTON));
```

35

You must process the WM_NOTIFY messages sent to the main window procedure in order to display the tool tips. You can use the same index (e.g., ID_NEW) for the commands and the strings, as in:

```
if(wMsg==WM_NOTIFY&&(HWND)lParam!=NULL)
{
LPTOOLTIPTEXT ttt;
static char bufr[64];
ttt=(LPTOOLTIPTEXT)lParam;
if(ttt->hdr.code==TTN_NEEDTEXT)
  {
  LoadString(hInst,ttt->hdr.idFrom,bufr,
sizeof(bufr));
  ttt->lpszText=bufr;
  SetWindowText(hMain,bufr);
  return(FALSE);
  }
}
```

If you want more elaborate buttons with more colors, different sizes, or irregular shapes, this requires a little more effort. In order to create your own buttons, there are four things you need to keep track of: 1) the state (pushed or not), 2) the command to send when it's pushed, 3) the tool tip or help text, and 4) the image to display. As it turns out, there are already enough extra variables for each window so that you don't need any additional data structures.

The same variable holds either the handle of the menu for a top-level window or the ID of a child window. You only need the low word of the ID, as the high word will be set to BN_CLICKED anyway. It only takes one bit to indicate whether the button is pushed or not. Use GetWindowLong() and SetWindowLong() with GWL_ID to access this information. This variable takes care of items 1 and 2.

The tool tip or help text is kept in the caption. Use GetWindowText() and SetWindowText() to access the tool tip or help text. Use CreateWindowEx() along with WS_EX_TOPMOST to create a bubble text window to display your tool tip. Set a timer to kill the window after some appropriate duration. This takes care of item 3.

Use SetWindowLong() and GetWindowLong() with GWL_USERDATA to store the image. This takes care of item 4. You will also need to register a class and create a procedure to draw the button and post commands when the button is pushed. Use DrawEdge() to create a raised or depressed appearance.

You can also use an additional bit with the ID to show the button as enabled or disabled. You don't have to maintain two separate bitmaps (one for enabled and a second for disabled), as the API used to paint the image will perform several different Raster OPerations (ROP), including a AND, XOR, NOT, etc. The following code snippet illustrates these techniques:

36

```
LRESULT WINAPI PushProc(HWND hWnd,UINT wMsg,WPARAM
    wParam,LPARAM lParam)
{
if(wMsg==WM_CLOSE)
   return(FALSE);
if(wMsg==WM_CREATE)
   return(FALSE);
if(wMsg==WM_DESTROY)
   return(FALSE);
if(wMsg==WM_LBUTTONDOWN)
   {
   if(GetWindowLong(hWnd,GWL_ID)&0x20000)
      {/* if enabled set pushed and redraw */
      SetWindowLong(hWnd,GWL_ID,
   GetWindowLong(hWnd,GWL_ID)|0x10000);
      InvalidateRect(hWnd,NULL,TRUE);
      }
   return(FALSE);
   }
if(wMsg==WM_LBUTTONUP)
   {
   if(GetWindowLong(hWnd,GWL_ID)&0x20000)
      {/* if enabled set not pushed and redraw */
      SetWindowLong(hWnd,GWL_ID,
   GetWindowLong(hWnd,GWL_ID)&0x2FFFF);
      InvalidateRect(hWnd,NULL,TRUE);
      PostMessage(GetParent(hWnd),WM_COMMAND,
   MAKEDWORD(GetWindowLong(hWnd,GWL_ID)&0xFFFF,
   BN_CLICKED),wMsg==WM_RBUTTONUP?1:0);
      }
   return(FALSE);
   }
if(wMsg==WM_PAINT)
   {
   BITMAPINFOHEADER*bh;
   BYTE*bi;
   DWORD ROP;
   HDC hDC;
   PAINTSTRUCT ps;
   RECT rc;
   hDC=BeginPaint(hWnd,&ps);
   GetClientRect(hWnd,&rc);
   FrameRect(hDC,&rc,GetBrush(BLACK));
   rc.left  +=1;
   rc.right -=1;
   rc.top   +=1;
   rc.bottom-=1;
   if(GetWindowLong(hWnd,GWL_ID)&0x10000)
      DrawEdge(hDC,&rc,EDGE_SUNKEN,BF_RECT);
```

```
        else
            DrawEdge(hDC,&rc,EDGE_RAISED,BF_RECT);
        rc.left   +=3;
        rc.right  -=3;
        rc.top    +=3;
        rc.bottom-=3;
        /* get pointer to bitmap */
        bh=(BITMAPINFOHEADER*)GetWindowLong(hWnd,
GWL_USERDATA);
        /* pointer to image (follows header and palette) */
        bi=(BYTE*)(((DWORD*)(((BYTE*)bh)+
sizeof(BITMAPINFOHEADER)))+(bm-
>biBitCount<24?(1<<bm->biBitCount):0));
        if(GetWindowLong(hWnd,GWL_ID)&0x20000)
            ROP=SRCCOPY; /* paint as enabled */
        else
            ROP=NOTSRCCOPY; /* paint as disabled */
        StretchDIBits(hDC,rc.left,rc.top,bh->biWidth,
bh->biHeight,0,0,bh->biWidth,bh->biHeight,bi,
(BITMAPINFO*)bh,DIB_RGB_COLORS,ROP);
        EndPaint(hWnd,&ps);
        return(FALSE);
        }
    return(DefWindowProc(hWnd,wMsg,wParam,lParam));
}
```

Chapter 6. Working with FONTs

The truth is that VB facilitates bad programming habits. Perhaps the simplest example of this is the ease with which the user can set the appearance of text in *forms* (i.e., what Windows® calls DIALOGs). Fonts were presented as the last of the *stock* objects in the chapter on *Objects and Controls*. Consider the following typical example of an about box which is in a VB application:

There are a total of 8 different fonts used in this example, only one of which is *stock*: the OK button and caption marked with a ✓. As stated in the description of FONTs, there are only 6 *stock* fonts. These are:

```
1) ANSI_FIXED_FONT
2) ANSI_VAR_FONT
3) DEVICE_DEFAULT_FONT
4) OEM_FIXED_FONT
5) SYSTEM_FIXED_FONT
6) SYSTEM_FONT
```

These are nominal descriptions. There is no guarantee that these will be different. Only one distinction is guaranteed: variable vs. fixed pitch. The 6 fonts listed above may be only 2. The variable pitch font is typically MS SansSerif before Vista® and Calibri on more recent versions. The fixed pitch font is typically Lucida Console or Courier New, but you can't be certain of this or of the font size, as these are all optional parameters in Windows®.

It is important to recognize that each of the text styles is a different font. Italic and bold are two separate fonts, as is bold italic. Serif and SanSerif are also separate fonts. Each size of text is a different font. Once a font is created the only thing you can change is the color.

Every time this about box is painted, these 7 fonts must be created and hopefully destroyed. If they are not destroyed, your application will continue to grow due to *memory leak.* You could create these 7 fonts once and save them,

39

but that would require additional structures and coding. Windows® does not check to see if a font already exists.

You might insist that the extra computational overhead is insignificant and not worth worrying about, since the box is only drawn once. Are you intentionally arguing for sloth? Computers are fast, so you can be lazy?

This about box may be drawn many times. If you drag it across the desktop, it will be repainted a hundred times. If it's obscured by another program (e.g., your screen saver), it will be repainted. If you minimize it (or select *Show Desktop*), it may be repainted a hundred more times. This is especially wasteful if you have *transitions* or *visual effects* enabled (see *Control Panel/ Display/ Advanced Settings*).

No, Windows® doesn't save a copy and use that to repaint.[5]

---

[5]There is a special class style, CS_SAVEBITS, but this doesn't apply to the entire DIALOG box above with all of its controls. Here's what Microsoft® has to say about this style:

> Saves, as a bitmap, the portion of the screen image obscured by a window. Windows uses the saved bitmap to re-create the screen image when the window is removed. Windows displays the bitmap at its original location and does not send WM_PAINT messages to windows obscured by the window if other screen actions have not invalidated the stored image. Use this style for small windows that are displayed briefly and then removed before other screen activity takes place (for example, menus or dialog boxes). This style increases the time required to display the window, because the operating system must first allocate memory to store the bitmap.

Chapter 7. Working with LISTBOXes

Windows® has only one type of stock list: the LISTBOX. This control has very limited capabilities: you can fill it with text and you can select one or more of these. It will sort the items and you can scroll it, but that's it. The COMBOBOX is a LISTBOX with an EDIT control that enables the user to change one of the items in the list, but that's all it does.

VB users are accustomed to list controls that have all the features of a database, because they <u>are</u> mustering a database from their application. Even the simplest lists in a VB application may be linked to an Access® database. The typical VB user finds this functionality useful, but it's like enlisting a surgeon, an anesthesiologist, and five nurses to peel a grape. VB may make this process less difficult, but it doesn't make it any less foolish.

The following code snippet illustrates how to create, fill, and process a list that the user can select from:

```
/* a list of planets */
char*Planets[]={
  "Mercury",
  "Venus",
  "Earth",
  "Mars",
  "Jupiter",
  "Saturn",
  "Uranus",
  "Neptune",
  "Pluto",
  NULL};

/* create and fill the list */
  hPlanets=CreateWindow("COMBOBOX",NULL,
    WS_CHILD|WS_VISIBLE|WS_CLIPSIBLINGS|
    CBS_DROPDOWNLIST|CBS_HASSTRINGS|WS_VSCROLL,
    left,top,wide,high,
    hParent,(HMENU)ID,hInst,NULL);
  for(i=0;Planets[i];i++)
    SendMessage(hPlanets,CB_ADDSTRING,0,
    (LPARAM)Planets[i]);

/* the message loop */
  while(GetMessage(&msg,NULL,0,0))
    if(msg.message==WM_COMMAND)
      if((HWND)msg.lParam==hPlanets)
        if(HIWORD(msg.wParam)==CBN_SELCHANGE||
          HIWORD(msg.wParam)==CBN_SELENDOK)
          a planet has been selected!
```

41

Chapter 8. Working with PROGRESS Controls

A PROGRESS extended control can be used to inform the user of a lengthy task or extended activity. The control includes only the sunken area and the blue spaces, as shown below. This control can be displayed on the application window. If you want the progress bar to pop up, you must create a top-level window with the WS_POPUP style and WS_EX_TOPMOST extended style and then create the PROGRESS bar as a child of this top-level window.

You must set the range and update the PROGRESS control, as illustrated below:

```
SendMessage(hPro1,PBM_SETRANGE,0,n);
for(i=0;i<n;i++)
  {
  /* perform extended activities */
  SendMessage(hPro1,PBM_SETPOS,i,0);
  }
```

As this is an extended control, don't forget to call InitCommonControls().

Chapter 9. Working with SCROLLBARs

All that's needed to add SCROLLBARS to a window is to add the style WS_HSCROLL and/or WS_VSCROLL when creating it. Windows® draws the SCROLLBARs for you, but it doesn't do anything with them and their position has no impact whatsoever on what's displayed in the window. All SCROLLBAR controls do is post messages when the user moves them. You must redraw what's in the window to reflect the changes. Except for sliding operations, you must redraw the SCROLLBARs too.

SCROLLBARs don't do anything but post messages.

After creating the window with the SCROLLBAR, you must set the range, which is just some convenient integer value, as illustrated below:

```
SetScrollRange(hWnd,SB_HORZ,0,bFile->biWidth-
    cR.right,FALSE);
```

Within your main the message loop you must process the WM_HSCROLL and WM_VSCROLL messages and every combination of parameters, as illustrated below:

```
if(wMsg==WM_HSCROLL)
    {
    int code,pmin,pmax,posi;
    code=LOWORD(wParam);
    GetScrollRange(hWnd,SB_HORZ,(int*)&pmin,
    (int*)&pmax);
    if(code==SB_LINELEFT)
        {
        posi=max(pmin,min(pmax,GetScrollPos(hWnd,
    SB_HORZ)-8));
        SetScrollPos(hWnd,SB_HORZ,posi,TRUE);
        }
    else if(code==SB_PAGELEFT)
        {
        posi=max(pmin,min(pmax,GetScrollPos(hWnd,
    SB_HORZ)-32));
        SetScrollPos(hWnd,SB_HORZ,posi,TRUE);
        }
    else if(code==SB_LINERIGHT)
        {
        posi=max(pmin,min(pmax,GetScrollPos(hWnd,SB_
    HORZ)+8));
        SetScrollPos(hWnd,SB_HORZ,posi,TRUE);
        }
    else if(code==SB_PAGERIGHT)
        {
        posi=max(pmin,min(pmax,GetScrollPos(hWnd,
    SB_HORZ)+32));
        SetScrollPos(hWnd,SB_HORZ,posi,TRUE);
        }
```

```
else if(code==SB_THUMBTRACK)
    {
    posi=max(pmin,min(pmax,HIWORD(wParam)));
    SetScrollPos(hWnd,SB_HORZ,posi,TRUE);
    }
/* force window to redraw */
InvalidateRect(hWnd,NULL,TRUE);
return(FALSE);
}
```

The call to InvalidateRect() forces the window to be redrawn. Before you redraw the window you must fetch the scrolling parameters, as illustrated below:

```
if(wMsg==WM_PAINT)
    {
    int hmin,hpos,hmax,vmin,vpos,vmax;
    HDC hDC;
    PAINTSTRUCT pS;
    hDC=BeginPaint(hWnd,&pS);

    GetScrollRange(hWnd,SB_HORZ,(int*)&hmin,(int*)&hmax);
    hpos=GetScrollPos(hWnd,SB_HORZ);

    GetScrollRange(hWnd,SB_VERT,(int*)&vmin,(int*)&vmax);
    vpos=GetScrollPos(hWnd,SB_VERT);

    /* redraw the window using scrolling parameters */

    EndPaint(hWnd,&pS);
    return(FALSE);
    }
```

Chapter 10. Working with STATUSBARs

STATUSBARs are very easy to use. You just create it and send it messages to change the text. Windows® takes care of positioning it and painting it. The size is set automatically. As this is an extended control, don't forget to call InitCommonControls().

```
hStatus=CreateWindow(STATUSCLASSNAME,"text",
 WS_CHILD|WS_VISIBLE|WS_BORDER,0,0,0,0,NULL,
 NULL,hInst,NULL);
SetWindowText(hStatus,"new text");
```

Chapter 11. Working with TABCONTROLs

TABCONTROLs are often used in Windows® applications, especially in Visual BASIC®. TABCONTROLs are easy to implement in Visual BASIC®, but not so in C. The following is a typical TABCONTROL:

| Exchanger Type | Constructional Details | Operating Conditions | Fluid Properties | Options | Low Fin Tubes |

Details & Dimensions

Number of Tube Passes 1

Number of Tubes 1

Tube Length 8   m

Tube ID 3.5   cm

☐ Low fin tubes

Tube OD 4.22   cm

Shell ID 0.0525   m

Tube Layout Square

Transverse Pitch 0   cm

Number of Baffles 0   Single segment

Baffle Cut 0   %

Tube Wall Therm. Cond. 65   W/m/°C

Pressure Loss Coefficients

Tube Side Ke 0   Kc 0

Shell Side Kf 0

Misc.

Lbb 0   cm

Ltb 0   cm

Lsb 0   cm

Nss 0

The TABCONTROL is an extended control, defined in commctrl.h and loaded with InitCommonControls(). Displaying a TABCONTROL isn't the problem. Hiding or showing and enabling or disabling all the other controls that sit on top of it is the problem. The only thing Windows® does for you is draw the row of text at the top and inform you when a user clicks on one of the tabs.

If you simply create a window with all of the controls shown above without understanding this, you would either have all of them on top of each other or not see any of them at all, depending on the order in which you created them. You must keep track of which controls are displayed with each tab.

Windows® does not do this for you.

The most efficient way to implement this is to create a separate GROUP box for each of the TABs. Create all of the GROUP boxes as children of the TABCONTROL, filling the client area of the TABCONTROL, as shown above by *Details & Dimensions*. All of the GROUP boxes will be on top of each other, but you control their visibility using ShowWindow() with either SW_SHOW or SW_HIDE so that only the one corresponding to the currently selected TAB is visible.

Then create all of the controls (e.g., STATIC, EDIT, and DROPDOWN) as children of the GROUP box that goes with each TAB. When the user selects a TAB, your mail loop will receive a message. Hide all of the GROUP boxes but one. When you hide a GROUP box, all of its children will also be hidden. This takes care of presenting the user with only those controls that go with the tab they have selected.

This logic will provide the necessary visibility of the controls, but doesn't handle the messages. The data entry (EDIT) and selection (DROPDOWN) controls will send messages to their parent loop, which will be one of the GROUP boxes. GROUP boxes are a type of BUTTON. Unless you subclass all buttons (*not recommended*) or provide your own procedure, your application loop will never see these messages and you won't know what the user has selected or entered. The GROUP boxes are children of the TABCONTROL, which is a child of the top-level window.

You must send the essential messages all the way back up through the inheritance tree to the application loop.

The following code snippet illustrates how to control the visibility of the children of a TABCONTROL.

```
if(wMsg==WM_NOTIFY&&(NMHDR*)lParam!=NULL)
{
HWND hTabs=((NMHDR*)lParam)->hwndFrom;
if(hTabs!=NULL)
  {
  UINT code=((NMHDR*)lParam)->code;
  if(code==TCN_SELCHANGE)
    {
    LRESULT selection=SendMessage(hTabs,
TCM_GETCURSEL,0,0);
      ShowWindow(hTab0,selection==0?SW_SHOW:SW_HIDE);
      ShowWindow(hTab1,selection==1?SW_SHOW:SW_HIDE);
      ShowWindow(hTab2,selection==2?SW_SHOW:SW_HIDE);
      ShowWindow(hTab3,selection==3?SW_SHOW:SW_HIDE);
    }
  return(FALSE);
  }
}
```

Chapter 12. Working with TREEVIEWs

TREEVIEW is a type of extended control. The most familiar example of this is the folder structure associated with selecting a file, but there are many other uses for this useful control. The following is an example:

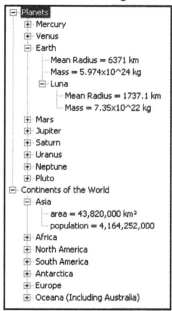

The contents of the list could come from many sources. In this example the contents come from a list of strings. The number of tabs at the beginning of each string controls the depth of the tree:

```
char*List[]={
    "Planets",
    "\tMercury",
    "\t\tMean Radius = 2439.7 km",
    "\t\tMass = 3.302x10^23 kg",
    "\tVenus",
    "\t\tMean Radius = 6051.8 km",
    "\t\tMass = 4.869x10^24 kg",
    "\tEarth",
    "\t\tMean Radius = 6371 km",
    "\t\tMass = 5.974x10^24 kg",
    "\t\tLuna",
    "\t\t\tMean Radius = 1737.1 km",
    "\t\t\tMass = 7.35x10^22 kg",
    "\tMars",
    "\t\tMean Radius = 3390 km",
    "\t\tMass = 6.419x10^23 kg",
```

```
"\t\tPhobos",
"\t\t\tMean Radius = 11.1 km",
"\t\t\tMass = 1.07x10^14 kg",
"\t\tDeimos",
"\t\t\tMean Radius = 6.3 km",
"\t\t\tMass = 2.0x10^15 kg",
"\tJupiter",
"\t\tMean Radius = 69911 km",
"\t\tMass = 1.899x10^27 kg",
"\t\tGanymede",
"\t\t\tMean Radius = 2631.2 km",
"\t\t\tMass = 1.482x10^23 kg",
"\t\tCallisto",
"\t\t\tMean Radius = 2410.3 km",
"\t\t\tMass = 1.076x10^23 kg",
"\t\tIo",
"\t\t\tMean Radius = 1821.5 km",
"\t\t\tMass = 8.93x10^22 kg",
"\t\tEuropa",
"\t\t\tMean Radius = 1561 km",
"\t\t\tMass = 4.8x10^22 kg",
"\t\t\tDensity = 3.01 g/cm³",
"\tSaturn",
"\t\tMean Radius = 58232 km",
"\t\tMass = 5.685x10^26 kg",
"\t\tTitan",
"\t\t\tType = Satellite of Saturn",
"\t\t\tMean Radius = 25766 km",
"\t\t\tMass = 1.345x10^23 kg",
"\t\tRhea",
"\t\t\tMean Radius = 764.11 km",
"\t\t\tMass = 2.317x10^21 kg",
"\t\tIapetus",
"\t\t\tMean Radius = 735.611 km",
"\t\t\tMass = 1.974x10^21 kg",
"\t\tDione",
"\t\t\tMean Radius = 561.6 km",
"\t\t\tMass = 1.096x10^21 kg",
"\t\tTethys",
"\t\t\tMean Radius = 533 km",
"\t\t\tMass = 6.173x10^20 kg",
"\t\tEnceladus",
"\t\t\tMean Radius = 252.1 km",
"\t\t\tMass = 1.08x10^20 kg",
"\t\tMimas",
"\t\t\tMean Radius = 198.3 km",
"\t\t\tMass = 3.749x10^19 kg",
"\tUranus",
"\t\tMean Radius = 25362 km",
```

```
"\t\tMass = 8.683x10^25 kg",
"\t\tTitania",
"\t\t\tMean Radius = 788.9 km",
"\t\t\tMass = 3.526x10^21 kg",
"\t\tOberon",
"\t\t\tMean Radius = 761.4 km",
"\t\t\tMass = 3.014x10^21 kg",
"\t\tUmbriel",
"\t\t\tMean Radius = 584.7 km",
"\t\t\tMass = 1.2x10^21 kg",
"\t\tAriel ",
"\t\t\tMean Radius = 578.9 km",
"\t\t\tMass = 1.35x10^21 kg",
"\t\tMiranda",
"\t\t\tMean Radius = 235.8 km",
"\t\t\tMass = 6.59x10^19 kg",
"\tNeptune",
"\t\tMean Radius = 24622 km",
"\t\tMass = 1.024x10^26 kg",
"\t\tTriton",
"\t\t\tMean Radius = 1353.4 km",
"\t\t\tMass = 2.15x10^22 kg",
"\t\tProteus",
"\t\t\tMean Radius = 210 km",
"\t\t\tMass = 5x10^19 kg",
"\tPluto",
"\t\tMean Radius = 11619 km",
"\t\tMass = 1.311x10^22 kg",
"\t\tCharon",
"\t\t\tMean Radius = 603.516 km",
"\t\t\tMass = 1.52x10^21 kg",
"Continents of the World",
"\tAsia",
"\t\tarea = 43,820,000 km²",
"\t\tpopulation = 4,164,252,000",
"\tAfrica",
"\t\tarea = 30,370,000 km²",
"\t\tpopulation = 1,022,234,000",
"\tNorth America",
"\t\tarea = 24,490,000 km²",
"\t\tpopulation = 542056000",
"\tSouth America",
"\t\tarea = 17,840,000 km²",
"\t\tpopulation = 392,555,000",
"\tAntarctica",
"\t\tarea = 13,720,000 km²",
"\t\tpopulation = 0",
"\tEurope",
"\t\tarea = 10,180,000 km²",
```

```
"\t\tpopulation = 738,199,000",
"\tOceana (Including Australia)",
"\t\tarea = 9,008,500 km²",
"\t\tpopulation = 29,127,000",
NULL};
```

The TREEVIEW control is complicated to implement and the available documentation is not always helpful. You must keep track of several thing about the content of your TREE, as in the following structure:

```
typedef struct{
    int max_depth;
    int ntree;
    char**list;
    HANDLE*Tree;
    HANDLE*Parent;
    HANDLE*hPrev;
}TREESTUFF;
```

You must first create the control, allocate memory for the data structure, save a pointer to the data structure in the USERDATA, and then fill the TREE. This next code snippet illustrates how to create the control up to the point of filling it:

```
InitCommonControls();
GetClientRect(hMain,&rc);
hTree=CreateWindow(WC_TREEVIEW,"",TVS_HASLINES|
    TVS_HASBUTTONS|TVS_LINESATROOT|TVS_HASLINES|
    WS_VISIBLE|WS_CHILD|WS_BORDER,left,top,wide,high,
    hMain,0,hInst,NULL);
treestuff=calloc(1,sizeof(TREESTUFF));
SetWindowLong(hTree,GWL_USERDATA,(LONG)treestuff);
FillTree(hTree,List);
```

Filling the TREE structure requires sending messages to the control and retrieving information returned after each message. This next code snippet illustrates this process:

```
void FillTree(HWND hTree,char**List)
{
int i,j,k;
TV_ITEM tvi;
TV_INSERTSTRUCT tvins;
TREESTUFF*treestuff;

treestuff=(TREESTUFF*)GetWindowLong(hTree,GWL_USERDAT
A);
SendMessage(hTree,TVM_DELETEITEM,0,(LPARAM)TVI_ROOT);
treestuff->list=List;
for(i=k=0;List[i];i++)
    {
    j=0;
```

```
while(List[i][j]=='\t')
   j++;
k=max(k,j);
}
treestuff->max_depth=k+1;
treestuff->hPrev=calloc(k+1,sizeof(HANDLE));
treestuff->ntree=i;
treestuff->Tree=calloc(i,sizeof(HANDLE));
treestuff->Parent=calloc(i,sizeof(HANDLE));
memset(&tvi,0,sizeof(tvi));
memset(&tvins,0,sizeof(tvins));
for(i=k=0;List[i];i++)
   {
   j=0;
   while(List[i][j]=='\t')
      j++;
   tvi.mask=TVIF_TEXT;
   tvi.pszText=List[i]+j;
   tvi.cchTextMax=strlen(tvi.pszText)+1;
   tvins.item=tvi;
   if(j>k)
      treestuff->hPrev[j]=NULL;
   tvins.hInsertAfter=treestuff->hPrev[j];
   if(j>0)
      tvins.hParent=treestuff->hPrev[j-1];
   else
      tvins.hParent=TVI_ROOT;
   treestuff->Parent[i]=tvins.hParent;
   treestuff-
>hPrev[j]=(HANDLE)SendMessage(hTree,TVM_INSERTITEM,0,
(LPARAM)&tvins);
   treestuff->Tree[i]=treestuff->hPrev[j];
   k=j;
   }
}
```

The TREEVIEW control also requires that you process messages. The messages tell you that the user has selected something and where this is on the TREE. You must keep track of whether the user has selected an item or moved the location in the TREE, for instance, expanding or collapsing it. TREEVIEW messages are problematic in 2 ways:

Note 1: The DBLCLK notification is not a TVN_xxx message; therefore, it doesn't return the handle of the item selected; and there is no TVN_DBLCLK message; so you have to save the item when it's selected and then use that handle when the DBLCLK message arrives.

Note 2: The TVGN_PARENT message is sent through the TVM_GETNEXTITEM message, which returns the parent of the next sibling rather than the parent of the current item. The TVGN_PREVIOUS is also sent through the TVM_GETNEXTITEM message so that it returns the current item, which doesn't get you any closer to getting the parent of the current item. This is why getting the parent of the current item is so complicated. If there is a TVN_GETTHISITEM message, it's not documented anywhere.

This next code snippet shows how you must process the messages in order to report that the user has selected something from your TREE:

```
if(wMsg==WM_NOTIFY)
{
int d,depth;
static TV_ITEM tvi;
HANDLE hItem;
NMHDR*nm;
NM_TREEVIEW*tv;
TREESTUFF*treestuff;
if((nm=(NMHDR*)lParam)!=NULL)
   {
   if(nm->code==NM_DBLCLK)
      {
      if(tvi.hItem)
         {
         treestuff=(TREESTUFF*)GetWindowLong(hTree,
GWL_USERDATA);
         hItem=tvi.hItem;
         depth=0;
         treestuff->hPrev[0]=hItem;
         while((hItem=GetParentHandle(hTree,hItem))
!=TVI_ROOT)
            {
            depth++;
            if(depth>=treestuff->max_depth)
              return(FALSE);
            treestuff->hPrev[depth]=hItem;
            }
         the user has selected this item!
         }
      }
   else if(nm->code==TVN_SELCHANGED)
      {
      tv=(NM_TREEVIEW*)lParam;
      if(tv)
         tvi=tv->itemNew;
      }
   }
return(FALSE);
}
```

56

Chapter 13. Working with Clipboard Data

There are several native data formats recognized by the Windows® clipboard. The two most common are BITMAP and TEXT. You can also register private formats and pass data back-and-forth between applications using the clipboard. The recommended method for passing data between applications is DDE.

Putting either of these two types of data onto the clipboard or retrieving it from the clipboard is fairly simple. The most important thing to remember is that you must put this data in a global memory object with a handle. This global memory object must have been allocated using the GlobalAlloc() function with the GMEM_MOVEABLE and GMEM_DDESHARE flags. Each line of text must also have both a CR and a LF and only one NUL at the very end.

This first code snippet illustrates putting text onto the clipboard:

```
void PutTextOnClipboard(char**text)
  {
  char*buf;
  int i,l;
  HGLOBAL hg;
  for(l=i=0;text[i];i++)
    l+=2+(int)strlen(text[i]);
  hg=GlobalAlloc(GMEM_MOVEABLE|GMEM_DDESHARE,l+1);
  buf=GlobalLock(hg);
  memset(buf,0,l+1);
  for(i=0;text[i];i++)
    {
    strcat(buf,text[i]);
    strcat(buf,"\r\n");
    }
  GlobalUnlock(hg)
  OpenClipboard(NULL);
  EmptyClipboard();
  SetClipboardData(CF_TEXT,hg);
  CloseClipboard();
  }
```

This second code snippet illustrates getting text from the clipboard:

```
char*GetTextFromClipboard()
  {
  char*ptr,*txt=NULL;
  HGLOBAL hg;
  if(IsClipboardFormatAvailable(CF_TEXT))
    {
    if(OpenClipboard(NULL))
      {
      if((hg=GetClipboardData(CF_TEXT))!=NULL)
        {
```

```
        if((ptr=GlobalLock(hg))!=NULL)
          {
          if((txt=malloc(strlen(ptr)+1))!=NULL)
            strcpy(txt,ptr);
          GlobalUnlock(hg);
          }
        }
      CloseClipboard();
      }
    }
  return(txt);
  }
```

This third code snippet illustrates putting a bitmap onto the clipboard:

```
void PutBitmapOnClipboard(BITMAPINFOHEADER*bm)
  {
  int l,w;
  BITMAPINFOHEADER*bg;
  HGLOBAL hg;
  w=4*((bm->biWidth*bm->biBitCount+31)/32);
  l=bm->biBitCount<24?(1<<bm->biBitCount):0;
  l=sizeof(BITMAPINFOHEADER)+l*sizeof(DWORD)+
    w*bm->biHeight;
  if((hg=GlobalAlloc(GMEM_MOVEABLE|GMEM_DDESHARE,l))
    !=NULL)
    {
    if((bg=GlobalLock(hg))!=NULL)
      memcpy(bg,bm,l);
    GlobalUnlock(hg);
    if(OpenClipboard(NULL))
      {
      EmptyClipboard();
      SetClipboardData(CF_DIB,hg);
      CloseClipboard();
      }
    }
  }
```

This fourth code snippet illustrates getting a bitmap from the clipboard:

```
BITMAPINFOHEADER*GetBitmapFromClipboard()
  {
  BITMAPINFOHEADER*bg,*bm=NULL;
  HGLOBAL hg;
  if(IsClipboardFormatAvailable(CF_DIB))
    {
    if(OpenClipboard(NULL))
      {
      if((hg=GetClipboardData(CF_DIB))!=NULL)
        {
        if((bg=GlobalLock(hg))!=NULL)
```

```
        {
        int l,w;
        w=4*((bg->biWidth*bg->biBitCount+31)/32);
        l=bg->biBitCount<24?(1<<bg->biBitCount):0;
        l=sizeof(BITMAPINFOHEADER)+l*sizeof(DWORD)
  +w*bg->biHeight;
        if((bm=malloc(l))!=NULL)
          memcpy(bm,bg,l);
        GlobalUnlock(hg);
        }
      }
    CloseClipboard();
      }
    }
return(bm);
}
```

Chapter 14. Performing a Screen Capture

There are at least two ways to perform a screen capture: 1) simulate pushing the PrtSc to copy what's on the screen to the clipboard and 2) getting the device context of the desktop and using BitBlt() to paint into a BITMAP. The first is described below:

An application can simulate a press of the PRINTSCREEN key in order to obtain a screen snapshot and save it to the Windows clipboard. To do this, call keybd_event with the bVirtualKey parameter set to VK_SNAPSHOT, and the bScanCode parameter set to 0 for a snapshot of the full screen or set bScanCode to 1 for a snapshot of the active window.

The following code snippet uses this method to capture the screen and save it to a file. The GetBitmapFromClipboard() function is in the previous chapter and the BMP32to24() function is provided in Appendix J.

```
void WriteBitmapToFile(BITMAPINFOHEADER*bm,char*fname)
{
FILE*fp;
static BITMAPFILEHEADER bf;
if((fp=fopen(fname,"wb"))!=NULL)
  {
  int l=(bm->biBitCount<24)?(1<<bm->biBitCount):0;
  l=sizeof(BITMAPINFOHEADER)+l*sizeof(DWORD);
  bf.bfOffBits=sizeof(BITMAPFILEHEADER)+l;
  bf.bfSize=bf.bfOffBits+bm->biSizeImage;
  bf.bfType=0x4D42;
  fwrite(&bf,1,sizeof(bf),fp);
  fwrite(bm,1,l+bm->biSizeImage,fp);
  fclose(fp);
  }
}
keybd_event(VK_SNAPSHOT,0,0,0);
if((bm=GetBitmapFromClipboard())!=NULL)
  {
  if(bm->biBitCount==32)
    BMP32to24(bm);
  WriteBitmapToFile(bm,fname);
  }
```

The following code snippet implements the second method described above:

```
BITMAPINFOHEADER*CopyDesktop()
{
int h,sh,si,w;
BITMAPINFOHEADER*bi;
BYTE*bits;
HDC hd,md;
HBITMAP hb;
w=GetSystemMetrics(SM_CXSCREEN);
```

61

```
h=GetSystemMetrics(SM_CYSCREEN);
si=(4*((w*24+31)/32))*h;
sh=sizeof(BITMAPINFOHEADER);
bi=calloc(sh+si,1);
bi->biSize=sizeof(BITMAPINFOHEADER);
bi->biBitCount=24;
bi->biPlanes=1;
bi->biWidth=w;
bi->biHeight=h;
bi->biSizeImage=si;
hd=GetDC(NULL);
md=CreateCompatibleDC(hd);
hb=CreateDIBSection(md,(BITMAPINFO*)bi,
  DIB_RGB_COLORS,&bits,NULL,0);
hb=SelectObject(md,hb);
BitBlt(md,0,0,w,h,hd,0,0,SRCCOPY);
memcpy(((BYTE*)bi)+sh,bits,si);
DeleteObject(hb);
DeleteDC(md);
return(bi);
}
```
If you use this second method and want to only capture part of the desktop, pass the desired coordinates to BitBlt().

Chapter 15. Charts & Graphs

Windows® doesn't draw charts or graphs. If you want a chart or graph, you must either use OLE (*not recommended*) or you must draw it yourself. What's more, you must draw every single detail of the chart, including the axis, numbers, tick marks, symbols, titles, and legends. Remember that each size and orientation (horizontal and vertical) is a different font.

You must draw every single detail of a chart yourself.

You must draw a chart or graph in a certain order so that the right parts are on top. Windows® doesn't order the parts for you, so you must paint bottom to top.

1) create fonts
2) create pens & brushes
3) draw title & axis labels
4) select appropriate axis increments (you must know how big the numbers will be on the Y-axis so as to leave the right amount of space for them)
5) determine the size of the plot area
6) draw the frame, grid, and axis divisions
7) draw the data (lines & symbols)
8) draw the legend
9) draw the axis numbers

If you always want the same font sizes, you can create the fonts and save them; otherwise, you will need to create, use, and then destroy them. You must create a new pen and/or brush for each color. Don't forget to destroy these when you're done with them.

Determining the best axis increments may require more lines of code than drawing the plot. Axis increments should be 1, 2, or 5 times some power of 10 (e.g., 0.1, 0.2, 0.5 or 100, 200, 500). You want to start and end at values that are some multiple of the increment. You want to have somewhere between 4 and 9 increments on the axis and the axis to span the range of the data. Meeting all of these criteria simultaneous may require an iterative solution and some creative programming.

If you want to plot logarithmic and probability axes, this will be even more complicated. Excel® does not plot probability axes, but such can be very useful. The cumulative normal probability distribution (i.e., the area under a bell-shaped curve) becomes a straight line when plotted on a probability axis. With a probability axis, you can see how close to or far from normally distributed the data are.

The increments on a probability axis are: 0.999, 0.99, 0.9, 0.8, 0.7, 0.6, 0.5, 0.4, 0.3, 0.2, 0.1, 0.01, and 0.001. The data transformation to the probability scale is based on $x=(1+erf(x'))/2$, where $erf()$ is the error function. The transformation is given by $x'=aprob(x)$ in the following code snippet.

63

```c
/* arc (inverse) probability function */
double aprob(double p)
  {
  double x,y,z;
  x=max(0.000001,min(0.999999,p));
  y=log10(x/(1.-x));
  z=y*y;
  return(((0.00346173*z+0.264988)*z+1.4365)*y/
    ((0.00675713*z+0.270504)*z+1.)/sqrt(2.));
  }
int StepSize(int axis,double*Amin,double*Astp,
    double*Amax,int inside)
  {
  int i,l,n,reverse;
  double Am,Ax,Step[]={10,20,50};
  if(axis==PROBABILITY)
    {
    if(Amin[0]<aprob(0.00001))
      return(-1);
    if(Amax[0]>aprob(0.99999))
      return(-1);
    i=0;
    while(aprob(pow(0.1,i))>Amin[0])
      i++;
    l=0;
    while(aprob(1.-pow(0.1,l))<Amax[0])
      l++;
    n=max(i,l);
    i=l=n;
    n=i+l+1;
    Amin[0]=aprob(pow(0.1,i));
    Amax[0]=aprob(1.-pow(0.1,l));
    Astp[0]=1;
    }
  else if(axis==LOGARITHMIC)
    {
    if(Amin[0]<-9.)
      return(-1);
    if(Amax[0]>9.)
      return(-1);
    i=(int)(Amin[0]+0.5);
    while(i>Amin[0])
      i--;
    Amin[0]=i;
    n=1-i;
    i=(int)(Amax[0]-0.5);
    while(i<Amax[0])
      i++;
    Amax[0]=i;
```

```
    Astp[0]=1;
    n+=i;
    }
else
    {
    if(Amin[0]>Amax[0])
      {
      reverse=1;
      Astp[0]=Amin[0];
      Amin[0]=Amax[0];
      Amax[0]=Astp[0];
      }
    else if(Amin[0]<Amax[0])
      reverse=0;
    else
      return(0);
    l=(int)(log10(Amax[0]-Amin[0])-3.);
    while(1)
      {
      for(i=0;i<3;i++)
        {
        Astp[0]=Step[i]*pow(10.,l);
        Am=Astp[0]*(int)(Amin[0]/(Astp[0]));
        while(Am<Amin[0])
          Am+=Astp[0];
        while(Am>Amin[0]+Astp[0]/1000.)
          Am-=Astp[0];
        Ax=Am;
        n=1;
        while(Ax<Amax[0]-Astp[0]/1000.)
          {
          Ax+=Astp[0];
          n++;
          if(n>9)
            break;
          }
        if(n<=9)
          goto end;
        }
      l++;
      }
    end:
    if(inside)
      {
      while(n>1&&Am<Amin[0]-(Amax[0]-Amin[0])/1000.)
        {
        Am+=Astp[0];
        n--;
        }
```
65

```
      while(n>1&&Am+(n-1)*Astp[0]>Amax[0]+(Amax[0]-
Amin[0])/1000.)
        {
        Ax-=Astp[0];
        n--;
        }
      }
    if(reverse)
      {
      Amin[0]=Ax;
      Amax[0]=Am;
      Astp[0]=-Astp[0];
      }
    else
      {
      Amin[0]=Am;
      Amax[0]=Ax;
      }
    }
  return(n);
  }
```

The following function draw the plot in the device context and rectangle passed to it:

```
void DrawPlot(HDC hDC,RECT rc)
  {
  char bufr[129],*buf;
  int
    a,i,j,k,p,legs,Nx,Ny,s,tall,x,x1,x2,x3,x4,y,y1,y2,y3,
    y4;
  double
    A,A1,A2,A3,A4,As,Ax,Ay,Bx,By,dX,dY,T,Ts,X,Xm,Xx,Y,Ym,
    Yx;
  HBRUSH hBrush;
  HFONT fBold,fHorz,fSymb,fVert;
  HPEN hPen;
  HRGN hClip;
  RECT pr;
  SIZE cs,sText,sTick,sXnum,sYnum;
    return;
  if(plot.sets<1)
    return;

  SetMapMode(hDC,MM_TEXT);

  tall=max(480,3*min(rc.right-rc.left,rc.bottom-
    rc.top)/4);
  fBold=CreateStandardFont("Arial",tall/28,FW_BOLD   ,
    0);
```

```
fHorz=CreateStandardFont("Arial",tall/32,FW_MEDIUM,
 0);
fSymb=CreateStandardFont("Arial",tall/32,FW_LIGHT ,
 0);
fVert=CreateStandardFont("Arial",tall/32,
 FW_MEDIUM,90);

/* white space inside black frame */
rc.left   +=tall/100;
rc.top    +=tall/100;
rc.right  -=tall/100;
rc.bottom-=tall/100;

SetTextColor(hDC,BLACK);
SetBkMode(hDC,TRANSPARENT);

hPen=CreatePen(PS_SOLID,1,BLACK);
hPen=SelectObject(hDC,hPen);

hBrush=CreateSolidBrush(BLACK);
hBrush=SelectObject(hDC,hBrush);

/* center title above plot */
SelectObject(hDC,fBold);
sText=GetTextSize(hDC,plot.Title);
TextOut(hDC,(rc.right+rc.left-sText.cx)/2,rc.top,
 plot.Title,(int)strlen(plot.Title));

/* center Y-axis label to left of plot */
SelectObject(hDC,fVert);
sText=GetTextSize(hDC,plot.Ylabel);
TextOut(hDC,rc.left,(rc.bottom+rc.top+
 sText.cx)/2,plot.Ylabel,(int)strlen(plot.Ylabel));

/* center X-axis label below plot */
SelectObject(hDC,fHorz);
sText=GetTextSize(hDC,plot.Xlabel);
TextOut(hDC,(rc.right+rc.left-sText.cx)/2,rc.bottom-
 sText.cy,plot.Xlabel,(int)strlen(plot.Xlabel));

A1=0.01;
A2=100.;
As=1.;
Ts=DBL_MAX;
for(a=0;a<32;a++)
  {
  if(a==31)
    A=As;
  else
```

67

```
   A=sqrt(A1*A2);
Xm=Ym=DBL_MAX;
Xx=Yx=-DBL_MAX;
for(i=s=0;s<plot.sets;s++)
   {
   for(p=0;p<plot.points[s];p++,i++)
      {
      if(plot.Xp[i]!=DBL_MAX&&plot.Yp[i]!=DBL_MAX)
         {
         Xm=min(Xm,plot.Xp[i]);
         Xx=max(Xx,plot.Xp[i]);
         Ym=min(Ym,plot.Yp[i]);
         Yx=max(Yx,plot.Yp[i]);
         }
      }
   }
if(Xm>=Xx)
   return;
if(Ym>=Yx)
   return;

if(A<1.)
   {
   dX=(Xx-Xm)*(1./A-1.);
   Xm-=dX/2.;
   Xx+=dX/2.;
   }
else
   {
   dY=(Yx-Ym)*(A-1);
   Ym-=dY/2.;
   Yx+=dY/2.;
   }

Nx=StepSize(plot.Xaxis,&Xm,&dX,&Xx,0);

SelectObject(hDC,fHorz);
sXnum.cx=sXnum.cy=0;
if(plot.Xaxis==PROBABILITY)
   {
   for(i=0;i<Nx;i++)
      {
      if(i<Nx/2)
         {
         X=pow(0.1,Nx/2-i);
         p=Nx/2-i;
         }
      else if(i>Nx/2)
         {
```

```
            X=1-pow(0.1,i-Nx/2);
            p=i-Nx/2;
            }
         else
            {
            X=0.5;
            p=1;
            }
         sprintf(bufr,"%*.*lf",p+2,p,X);
         sText=GetTextSize(hDC,bufr);
         sXnum.cx=max(sXnum.cx,sText.cx);
         sXnum.cy=max(sXnum.cy,sText.cy);
         }
      }
   else
      {
      for(X=Xm;X<=Xx+dX/10;X+=dX)
         {
         sText=GetTextSize(hDC,AxisNumber(plot.Xaxis,
Xm,Xx,X));
         sXnum.cx=max(sXnum.cx,sText.cx);
         sXnum.cy=max(sXnum.cy,sText.cy);
         }
      }

   Ny=StepSize(plot.Yaxis,&Ym,&dY,&Yx,0);

   sYnum.cx=sYnum.cy=0;
   if(plot.Yaxis==PROBABILITY)
      {
      for(i=0;i<Ny;i++)
         {
         if(i<Ny/2)
            {
            Y=pow(0.1,Ny/2-i);
            p=Ny/2-i;
            }
         else if(i>Ny/2)
            {
            Y=1-pow(0.1,i-Ny/2);
            p=i-Ny/2;
            }
         else
            {
            Y=0.5;
            p=1;
            }
         sprintf(bufr,"%*.*lf",p+2,p,Y);
         sText=GetTextSize(hDC,bufr);
```

69

```
        sYnum.cx=max(sYnum.cx,sText.cx);
        sYnum.cy=max(sYnum.cy,sText.cy);
        }
    }
  else
    {
    for(Y=Ym;Y<=Yx+dY/10;Y+=dY)
      {
      sText=GetTextSize(hDC,A
xisNumber(plot.Yaxis,Ym,Yx,Y));
      sYnum.cx=max(sYnum.cx,sText.cx);
      sYnum.cy=max(sYnum.cy,sText.cy);
      }
    }

  sTick=GetTextSize(hDC,"0");

  pr.left   =rc.left   +3*sTick.cx+sYnum.cx;
  pr.top    =rc.top    +5*sXnum.cy/4;
  pr.right  =rc.right  -sXnum.cx/2;
  pr.bottom=rc.bottom-sXnum.cy-sYnum.cy;

  Ax=(pr.right-pr.left)/(Xx-Xm);
  Ay=(pr.bottom-pr.top)/(Yx-Ym);
  Bx=pr.left-Ax*Xm;
  By=pr.bottom+Ay*Ym;

  if(!plot.aspect)
    break;

  T=fabs(Ax-Ay);
  if(T<Ts)
    {
    As=A;
    Ts=T;
    }
  if(Ax<Ay)
    A1=A;
  else
    A2=A;
  }

if(plot.Xaxis==PROBABILITY)
  {
  for(i=0;;i++)
    {
    if(i<Nx/2)
      {
      X=pow(0.1,Nx/2-i);
```
70

```
      p=Nx/2-i;
      }
   else if(i>Nx/2)
      {
      X=1-pow(0.1,i-Nx/2);
      p=i-Nx/2;
      }
   else
      {
      X=0.5;
      p=1;
      }
   sprintf(bufr,"%*.*lf",p+2,p,X);
   x=nint(Bx+Ax*aprob(X));
   sText=GetTextSize(hDC,bufr);
   TextOut(hDC,x-sText.cx/2,pr.bottom+
sTick.cx/4,bufr,(int)strlen(bufr));
   DrawLine(hDC,x,pr.bottom+sTick.cx/4,x,pr.top-
sTick.cx/2);
   if(i==Nx-1)
      break;
   if(X<0.09)
      {
      for(k=2;k<=9;k++)
         {
         x=nint(Bx+Ax*(aprob(X*k)));
         DrawLine(hDC,x,pr.bottom-
sTick.cx/2,x,pr.bottom);
         DrawLine(hDC,x,pr.top,x,pr.top+sTick.cx/2);
         }
      }
   else if(X<0.4)
      {
      for(k=2;k<=4;k++)
         {
         x=nint(Bx+Ax*(aprob(k/10.)));
         DrawLine(hDC,x,pr.bottom-
sTick.cx/2,x,pr.bottom);
         DrawLine(hDC,x,pr.top,x,pr.top+sTick.cx/2);
         }
      }
   else if(X<0.8)
      {
      for(k=6;k<=8;k++)
         {
         x=nint(Bx+Ax*(aprob(k/10.)));
         DrawLine(hDC,x,pr.bottom-
sTick.cx/2,x,pr.bottom);
         DrawLine(hDC,x,pr.top,x,pr.top+sTick.cx/2);
```

71

```
          }
        }
      else
        {
        for(k=2;k<=9;k++)
          {
          x=nint(Bx+Ax*(aprob(X+(1.-X)*k/10.)));
          DrawLine(hDC,x,pr.bottom-
sTick.cx/2,x,pr.bottom);
          DrawLine(hDC,x,pr.top,x,pr.top+sTick.cx/2);
          }
        }
      }
    }
  else
    {
    for(X=Xm;;X+=dX)
      {
      x=nint(Bx+Ax*X);
      buf=AxisNumber(plot.Xaxis,Xm,Xx,X);
      sText=GetTextSize(hDC,buf);
      TextOut(hDC,x-sText.cx/2,pr.bottom+
sTick.cx/4,buf,(int)strlen(buf));
      DrawLine(hDC,x,pr.bottom+sTick.cx/4,x,pr.top-
sTick.cx/2);
      if(X+dX>Xx+dX/10.)
         break;
      if(plot.Xaxis==LOGARITHMIC)
        {
        for(k=2;k<=9;k++)
          {
          x=nint(Bx+Ax*(X+log10(k)));
          DrawLine(hDC,x,pr.bottom-
sTick.cx/2,x,pr.bottom);
          DrawLine(hDC,x,pr.top,x,pr.top+sTick.cx/2);
          }
        }
      else
        {
        for(k=1;k<5;k++)
          {
          x=nint(Bx+Ax*(X+k*dX/5.));
          DrawLine(hDC,x,pr.bottom-
sTick.cx/2,x,pr.bottom);
          DrawLine(hDC,x,pr.top,x,pr.top+sTick.cx/2);
          }
        }
      }
    }
  }
```

```c
if(plot.Yaxis==PROBABILITY)
  {
  for(i=0;;i++)
    {
    if(i<Ny/2)
      {
      Y=pow(0.1,Ny/2-i);
      p=Ny/2-i;
      }
    else if(i>Ny/2)
      {
      Y=1-pow(0.1,i-Ny/2);
      p=i-Ny/2;
      }
    else
      {
      Y=0.5;
      p=1;
      }
    sprintf(bufr,"%*.*lf",p+2,p,Y);
    y=nint(By-Ay*aprob(Y));
    sText=GetTextSize(hDC,bufr);
    TextOut(hDC,pr.left-sText.cx-3*sTick.cx/4,y-
sText.cy/2,bufr,(int)strlen(bufr));
    DrawLine(hDC,pr.left-
sTick.cx/2,y,pr.right+sTick.cx/4,y);
    if(i==Ny-1)
      break;
    if(Y<0.09)
      {
      for(k=2;k<=9;k++)
        {
        y=nint(By-Ay*(aprob(Y*k)));
        DrawLine(hDC,pr.left,y,pr.left+sTick.cx/2,y);
        DrawLine(hDC,pr.right-
sTick.cx/2,y,pr.right,y);
        }
      }
    else if(Y<0.4)
      {
      for(k=2;k<=4;k++)
        {
        y=nint(By-Ay*(aprob(k/10.)));
        DrawLine(hDC,pr.left,y,pr.left+sTick.cx/2,y);
        DrawLine(hDC,pr.right-
sTick.cx/2,y,pr.right,y);
        }
      }
```

```
    else if(Y<0.8)
        {
        for(k=6;k<=8;k++)
            {
            y=nint(By-Ay*(aprob(k/10.)));
            DrawLine(hDC,pr.left,y,pr.left+sTick.cx/2,y);
            DrawLine(hDC,pr.right-
sTick.cx/2,y,pr.right,y);
            }
        }
    else
        {
        for(k=2;k<=9;k++)
            {
            y=nint(By-Ay*(aprob(Y+(1.-Y)*k/10.)));
            DrawLine(hDC,pr.left,y,pr.left+sTick.cx/2,y);
            DrawLine(hDC,pr.right-
sTick.cx/2,y,pr.right,y);
            }
        }
    }
else
    {
    for(Y=Ym;;Y+=dY)
        {
        y=nint(By-Ay*Y);
        buf=AxisNumber(plot.Yaxis,Ym,Yx,Y);
        sText=GetTextSize(hDC,buf);
        TextOut(hDC,pr.left-sText.cx-3*sTick.cx/4,y-
sText.cy/2,buf,(int)strlen(buf));
        DrawLine(hDC,pr.left-
sTick.cx/2,y,pr.right+sTick.cx/4,y);
        if(Y+dY>Yx+dY/10.)
            break;
        if(plot.Yaxis==LOGARITHMIC)
            {
            for(k=2;k<=9;k++)
                {
                y=nint(By-Ay*(Y+log10(k)));
                DrawLine(hDC,pr.left,y,pr.left+sTick.cx/2,y);
                DrawLine(hDC,pr.right-
sTick.cx/2,y,pr.right,y);
                }
            }
        else
            {
            for(k=1;k<5;k++)
                {
```

```
            y=nint(By-Ay*(Y+k*dY/5.));
            DrawLine(hDC,pr.left,y,pr.left+sTick.cx/2,y);
            DrawLine(hDC,pr.right-
      sTick.cx/2,y,pr.right,y);
            }
          }
        }
      }

   rc.left   =pr.left   -1;
   /* clip drawing to plot area */
   rc.bottom=pr.bottom+1;
   rc.right  =pr.right  +1;
   rc.top    =pr.top    -1;
   hClip=CreateRectRgn(rc.left,rc.top,
    rc.right,rc.bottom);
   SelectClipRgn(hDC,hClip);

   SelectObject(hDC,fSymb);

   for(i=s=0;s<plot.sets;i+=plot.points[s++])
     {
     SetTextColor(hDC,RGB2BGR(plot.color[s]));

     hPen=SelectObject(hDC,hPen);
     DeleteObject(hPen);
     hPen=CreatePen(PS_SOLID,1,RGB2BGR(plot.color[s]));
     hPen=SelectObject(hDC,hPen);

     hBrush=SelectObject(hDC,hBrush);
     DeleteObject(hBrush);
     hBrush=CreateSolidBrush(RGB2BGR(plot.color[s]));
     hBrush=SelectObject(hDC,hBrush);

     if(plot.type[s]&POLYGON)
       {
       POINT*pt;
       pt=allocate(__LINE__,plot.points[s],
    sizeof(POINT));
       j=i;
       for(p=k=0;p<plot.points[s];p++,j++)
         {
         if(plot.Xp[j]!=DBL_MAX&&plot.Yp[j]!=DBL_MAX)
           {
           pt[p].x=nint(Bx+Ax*plot.Xp[j]);
           pt[p].y=nint(By-Ay*plot.Yp[j]);
           k++;
           }
         }
```

```
      Polygon(hDC,pt,k);
      release(__LINE__,pt);
      }
   if(plot.type[s]&SYMBOL)
      {
      j=i;
      for(p=0;p<plot.points[s];p++,j++)
         {
         if(plot.Xp[j]!=DBL_MAX&&plot.Yp[j]!=DBL_MAX)
            {
            x=nint(Bx+Ax*plot.Xp[j]);
            y=nint(By-Ay*plot.Yp[j]);
            DrawSymbol(hDC,plot_
symbols[s%((int)strlen(plot_symbols))],x,y);
            }
         }
      }
   if(plot.type[s]&VECTOR)
      {
      As=Ay/Ax;
      Ts=-DBL_MAX;
      j=i;
      for(p=0;p<plot.points[s];p++,j++)
         if(plot.Xp[j]!=DBL_MAX&&plot.Yp[j]!=DBL_MAX)
            Ts=max(Ts,_hypot(plot.Up[p],As*plot.Vp[j]));
      if(Ts<FLT_EPSILON)
         return;
      j=i;
      for(p=0;p<plot.points[s];p++,j++)
         {
         if(plot.Xp[j]!=DBL_MAX&&plot.Yp[j]!=DBL_MAX)
            {
            x1=nint(Bx+Ax*plot.Xp[j]);
            y1=nint(By-Ay*plot.Yp[j]);
            T=_hypot(plot.Up[j],As*plot.Vp[j]);
            if(T>0.)
               A=atan2(As*plot.Vp[j],plot.Up[j]);
            else
               A=0.;
            A3=A+4.*M_PI/5.;
            A4=A-4.*M_PI/5.;
            x2=x1+nint(tall*cos(A)/40.*T/Ts);
            y2=y1-nint(tall*sin(A)/40.*T/Ts);
            x3=x2+nint(tall*cos(A3)/160.);
            y3=y2-nint(tall*sin(A3)/160.);
            x4=x2+nint(tall*cos(A4)/160.);
            y4=y2-nint(tall*sin(A4)/160.);
            DrawLine(hDC,x1,y1,x2,y2);
            DrawLine(hDC,x3,y3,x2,y2);
```

```
                DrawLine(hDC,x2,y2,x4,y4);
              }
          }
      }
    if(plot.type[s]&CURVE)
      {
      j=i;
      x2=nint(Bx+Ax*plot.Xp[j]);
      y2=nint(By-Ay*plot.Yp[j]);
      for(p=1;p<plot.points[s];p++)
        {
        x1=x2;
        y1=y2;
        j++;
        x2=nint(Bx+Ax*plot.Xp[j]);
        y2=nint(By-Ay*plot.Yp[j]);
        if(plot.Xp[j-1]!=DBL_MAX&&plot.Yp[j-1]!=DBL_MAX)
          if(plot.Xp[j]!=DBL_MAX&&plot.Yp[j]!=DBL_MAX)
            DrawLine(hDC,x1,y1,x2,y2);
        }
      }
    }

if(!plot.position)
  goto the_end;

SetBkMode(hDC,OPAQUE);
SelectObject(hDC,fHorz);

for(x=y=s=legs=0;s<plot.sets;s++)
  {
  if(plot.legend[s])
    {
    if(strlen(plot.legend[s]))
      {
      cs=GetTextSize(hDC,plot.legend[s]);
      x=max(x,cs.cx);
      y=max(y,cs.cy);
      legs++;
      }
    }
  }

if(plot.position==LOWER_LEFT)
  {
  x=pr.left+sTick.cx;
  y=pr.bottom-(2*legs+1)*sTick.cy/2;
  }
else if(plot.position==LOWER_RIGHT)
```

77

```
      {
      x=pr.right-x-sTick.cx;
      y=pr.bottom-(2*legs+1)*sTick.cy/2;
      }
   else if(plot.position==UPPER_LEFT)
      {
      x=pr.left+sTick.cx;
      y=pr.top+sTick.cy/2;
      }
   else if(plot.position==UPPER_RIGHT)
      {
      x=pr.right-x-sTick.cx;
      y=pr.top+sTick.cy/2;
      }
   else
      return;

   for(s=0;s<plot.sets;s++)
      {
      if(plot.legend[s])
         {
         if(strlen(plot.legend[s]))
            {
            SetTextColor(hDC,RGB2BGR(plot.color[s]));
            TextOut(hDC,x,y,plot.legend[s],
   (int)strlen(plot.legend[s]));
            y+=sXnum.cy;
            }
         }
      }

   the_end:
   DeleteObject(fBold);
   DeleteObject(fHorz);
   DeleteObject(fSymb);
   DeleteObject(fVert);

   DeleteObject(hClip);

   hPen=SelectObject(hDC,hPen);
   DeleteObject(hPen);

   hBrush=SelectObject(hDC,hBrush);
   DeleteObject(hBrush);
   }
```
Some colors and symbols that work well in plots are listed below:
```
#define blue         0x0000FF
#define brass        0xA67D3D
#define bronze       0x8F7F5F
```

```
#define brown          0x7F3F00
#define copper         0xD98719
#define cyan           0x00FFFF
#define dark_cyan      0x008B8B
#define forest_green   0x1F7F1F
#define gold           0xFFD700
#define green          0x00FF00
#define magenta        0xFF00FF
#define navy_blue      0x00007F
#define orange         0xFF7F00
#define red            0xFF0000
#define violet         0x9400D3
#define yellow         0xFFFF00

#define RGB2BGR(rgb)
    (((rgb&0xFF)<<16)|(rgb&0xFF00)|(rgb&0xFF0000)>>16)

DWORD plot_colors[16]={blue,red,green,brown,copper,
    gold,dark_cyan,forest_green,cyan,magenta,brass,
    navy_blue,orange,bronze,violet,yellow};

char*plot_symbols="*+@#¤¥§©®±µ»÷øabcdefghijklmnopqrstuvw
    xyz$%&†‡Š™¢ABCDEFGHIJKLMNOPQRSTUVWXYZ";
```

Chapter 16. Making it all Fit on the Screen

It is very frustrating to open an application that only works correctly if you happen to have the same size and aspect display as the developer. I have opened several such applications where the initial form is so large that the buttons–including the Exit button–are down off the bottom of the display and can't be seen, let alone pushed to close it.

There's no excuse for such ignorance or apathy.

There are several things you need to do to control the size and position of your applications. The first of these is in the window creation process. The first message your main procedure will receive when the application window is created is WM_CREATE. You must return FALSE to continue with the process. This first code snippet shows how to appropriately size and center the application window on the display. In this case the application will fill 3/4ths of the display.

```
if(wMsg==WM_CREATE)
{
int h,high,w,wide;
wide=GetSystemMetrics(SM_CXSCREEN);
high=GetSystemMetrics(SM_CYSCREEN);
w=3*wide/4;
h=3*high/4;
MoveWindow(hWnd,(wide-w)/2,(high-h)/2,w,h,TRUE);
return(FALSE);
}
```

This next code snippet illustrates how to set the minimum size so that everything will still fit, in this case 640x480. It also shows when you need to resize and/or reposition all of the controls because the user has changed the size of the application window:

```
if(wMsg==WM_GETMINMAXINFO)
{
MINMAXINFO*mInfo=(MINMAXINFO*)lParam;
mInfo->ptMinTrackSize.x=640;
mInfo->ptMinTrackSize.y=480;
return(FALSE);
}
if(wMsg==WM_SIZE)
{
if(wParam==SIZE_MAXIMIZED||wParam==SIZE_RESTORED)
  ResizeWindows();
return(FALSE);
}
```

The following is an example of an application that requires the controls to be resized when the size of the main window is changed:

81

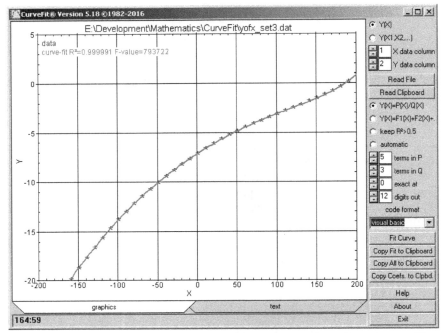

The spacing between the controls and buttons must be adjusted, as well as the position of the TAB and STATUSBAR controls. This next code snippet illustrates how to implement this.

```
SIZE GetTextSize(HDC hdc,char*text)
   {
   static SIZE st;
   GetTextExtentPoint32(hdc,text,(int)strlen(text),&st);
   return(st);
   }

void ResizeWindows()
   {
   char text[32];
   int a=24,h,i,p,w,x,y;
   HDC hdc;
   RECT rc;
   SIZE st,sx;
   if(IsIconic(hMain))
      return;

   /* determine size of text (This isn't the same on
      every display and you'll need it to size the buttons
      correctly.) */
   hdc=GetDC(hMain);
```

82

```
SelectObject(hdc,GetStockObject(ANSI_VAR_FONT));
for(sx.cx=sx.cy=i=0;Push[i].name;i++)
   {
   sprintf(text,"***%s***",Push[i].name);
   st=GetTextSize(hdc,text);
   sx.cx=max(sx.cx,st.cx);
   sx.cy=max(sx.cy,st.cy);
   }
ReleaseDC(hMain,hdc);

/* get size of client area */
GetClientRect(hMain,&rc);

/* determine the width of the right panel */
w=max(bLogo->biWidth,sx.cx)+2;
h=bLogo->biHeight+2;
p=3*sx.cy/2;
x=rc.right-1-w;
y=1;

/* position the logo */
MoveWindow(hLogo,x,y,bLogo->biWidth,bLogo-
  >biHeight,TRUE);

/* position the buttons */
y+=h+2;
for(i=0;Push[i].name;i++,y+=3*sx.cy/2+2)
   MoveWindow(Push[i].hWnd,x,y,w,3*sx.cy/2,TRUE);
}
```

Chapter 17. Acronyms

API: Application Programming Interface
BASIC: Beginner's All-Purpose Symbolic Instruction Code
DDE: Dynamic Data Exchange
DLL: Dynamic Link Library
DIB: Device Independent Bitmap
FORTRAN: FORmula TRANslator
GDI: Graphic Display Interface
GUI: Graphical User Interface
OCX: OLE Control eXtension
OLE: Object Linking and Embedding

Appendix A: C Compilers

Everything you need to build applications written in C for the Windows® operating system can be obtained without cost. There are several compilers that you can find on the Internet. They each have different strengths and weaknesses.

The Microsoft® C Compiler

Go to www.microsoft.com or search for "SDK download." I recommend Version 7.0A or 7.1 of the Software Development Kit. You will also need Version 7.0 of the Driver Development Kit (DDK). These are both free downloads.

Microsoft® Visual Studio® is an Interactive Development and Debugging Environment (IDDE) and is entirely superfluous. The C compiler, resource compiler, and linker all come with the SDK and DDK, so there's no point purchasing Visual Studio®.

Just say NO to Visual Studio®.

Download any one of the many free text editors available online and write a two-line batch file to compile and link your application. The first line below launches the resource compiler and the second launches the C compiler as well as the linker. This is all it takes to build an application.

```
rc myprog.rc
cl myprog.c myprog.res user32.lib gdi32.lib
```

The DDK also includes a cross-compiler. This allows you to create 64-bit applications on a 32-bit machine. You'll find this compiler in a folder named ...\bin\x86\amd64\. You can also build 32-bit applications on a 64-bit machine. You'll find that compiler in a folder named, ...\bin\amd64\x86\. Keep the two compilers in separate folders. Either compiler can be conveniently selected with a short batch file, as in the following:

```
SET BIN=C:\VC64\BIN
SET LIB=.;C:\VC64\LIB
SET PATH=C:\VC64\BIN; %windir%\SYSTEM32;%windir%
SET INCLUDE=.;C:\VC64\INCLUDE
```

The Digital Mars C Compiler

Walter Bright wrote the first ever single-pass C++ compiler. It was called Zortech®. Symantec® picked it up for several years but dumped it when they realized it wasn't profitable. Walter Bright retained the rights and you can now download this excellent compiler for free off the Internet.

Walter Bright is a genius!

The Digital Mars C compiler will only create 32-bit native executables. There are no plans at this time to add 64-bit capability. You don't really need 64-bit executables except for Excel Add-Ins. If you have a 64-bit copy of MSOffice® you must also have a 64-bit compiler and linker in order to create compatible Add-Ins for it.

87

Walter Bright's compilers don't optimize code as tightly as the Microsoft® compiler, but it is much more reliable. For the first two decades of its existence, the Microsoft® *optimizing* C compiler was very slow and buggy. There have been considerable improvements in the past decade so that it is now faster and more reliable.

The most amazing feature of Walter Bright's compilers is the *generate trace* functionality that is activated with the -gt option. When this option is activated the application runs very slowly, but when it's done, it leaves behind a list (TRACE.LOG) of every function, how many times it was called, by what other function, and how long it took. You can use this information to optimize and structure your code.

If you run the application again without deleting this file, it will accumulate the sums. This marvelous feature that Walter Bright has built into his compilers requires no additional effort on your part. You will be surprised to discover that for most applications a few functions completely dominate the runtime.

Other C Compilers

While some of the Gnu® tools and code can be made to function on the Windows® platform, you will find this quite a hassle. Everything Gnu® is developed within an entirely different framework. It can be done, but you will waste a lot of time doing it.

The Intel® compiler was free at one time, but now costs $699. Unless you're specifically developing applications for parallel processing there's no point, especially when other compilers are available for free. The optimization features that come with the Intel® compiler are useful, but nothing can come close to Walter Bright's -gt!

Appendix B: The .Net Framework®

According to Microsoft®, "the .NET Framework is a technology that supports building and running the next generation of applications and XML Web services. The .NET Framework is designed to fulfill the following objectives:

•To provide a consistent object-oriented programming environment whether object code is stored and executed locally, executed locally but Internet-distributed, or executed remotely.

•To provide a code-execution environment that minimizes software deployment and versioning conflicts.

•To provide a code-execution environment that promotes safe execution of code, including code created by an unknown or semi-trusted third party.

•To provide a code-execution environment that eliminates the performance problems of scripted or interpreted environments.

•To make the developer experience consistent across widely varying types of applications, such as Windows-based applications and Web-based applications.

•To build all communication on industry standards to ensure that code based on the .NET Framework can integrate with any other code."

The .Net Framework® is a code management system developed by Microsoft® that runs on top of the Windows® operating system. The official reasons given for the .Net Framework® are to improve portability, reliability, consistency, and security. Of course, it does none of these things. In spite of it's being released almost 14 years ago, code written for the .Net Framework® is still not compatible with any other operating system besides Windows®.

C# is Microsoft's *special* language that targets the .Net Framework®. This phrase *target's the .Net Framework* is significant. What this means is that, after you compile and link your program, it produces what's called *managed code* rather than a stand-alone (or *native*) executable.

The important thing to remember about VB.Net® and C# is that you can only produce *managed code*. You cannot produce a stand-alone executable. *Managed code* will always be problematic and much slower due to the *management* overhead plus an additional abstraction layer between the code and the machine.

The term *managed code* is much more insidious than mere inefficiency. It means that your code is exposed for the entire world to see. Red-Gate® Software sells a tool called .Net Reflector®. If you open any .Net executable created by Visual Studio .Net® with this tool, it will display the source code. You can select the format to display: VB.Net®, C#, or F#. Red-Gate offers a 14-day free trial, so that anyone can recover your .Net source code without paying a cent.

Just say NO to the .Net Framework®.

89

Native Executable	Managed Code
fast and efficient	slower than a herd of snails stampeding up the side of a salt dome in a hailstorm
can be made independent of O/S version, service pack, drivers, and DLLs	always dependent on O/S version, service packs, drivers, and DLLs
raw (uncooked) code execution	half-baked layer of *management* between your code and the O/S
third-party drivers can be eliminated	endless problems with third-party drivers

Appendix C: Visual BASIC®

Several development systems and coding languages are referred to as Visual BASIC®. All are products of Microsoft®. The original–simply referred to as VB–was an extension of BASIC (Beginner's All-Purpose Symbolic Instruction Code) that provided GUI capability on the Windows® operating system. Visual BASIC for Applications® (VBA) is the subset of VB used to create macros in MSWord®, Excel®, and other Microsoft® applications. VB.Net® is the version of VB that targets the .Net Framework®.

Visual BASIC® 1.0 was released in 1991. The final version of VB was 6.0, which was released in 1998. Since that time all of the releases have been .Net. The exposure associated with all *managed code* makes VB entirely unsuitable. You can no longer create native executables from VB code. There is no sufficiently compelling reason to develop anything in VB.

The advantage of VB has always been that you could quickly build small applications that had surprisingly good interactive features. The development system (Visual Studio®) facilitates the utilization of very powerful controls, including: complex lists, formatted text, charts, database functions, and more. These useful features are also the source of perpetual compatibility issues.

Just say NO to Visual Basic®.

Appendix D: Linear vs. Object-Oriented Code

There are two distinct approaches to software development that arise from structure: linear and object-oriented coding. VB.Net®, C#, and C++ are designed for object-oriented code. C, Pascal, BASIC, and FORTRAN are not.

Linear Code	Object-Oriented Code
structured approach	unstructured team approach (think: herding cats)
the work of a small, highly disciplined team	huge investment in manpower to develop and maintain (think: it takes a village)
easier to identify and fix bugs	difficult to identify and fix bugs
at least one person *must* know how it all fits together	no one person knows how it all fits together

No matter what language you employ to write code or what structure you build, eventually it will end up as machine instructions. There's no such thing as object-oriented machine language. Processors don't operate on objects. They merely execute individual instructions–that is, linear code.

Processors only operate on linear code.

There are many more reasons to avoid object-oriented code than those listed in the table above. Perhaps the most disturbing is the casual use of exceptions. Would you pull the fire alarm to have a pizza delivered? Sounds crazy, doesn't it? But this is a routine practice in VB.Net, C++, and C# programming. It's called *throwing* and *catching* exceptions and is an integral part of object-oriented programming.

The pizza place may be next door to the fire station and the guys with the big red truck could pick up one on the way to your house (that's not really on fire), but you shouldn't use the fire department to deliver pizza. This is like shouting, "Fire!" in a crowded theater just to get a particular seat. You could dig a ditch with old nuclear warheads, but a backhoe will get the job done without contaminating the area.

Exceptions should be reserved for critical events, including: stack overflow and underflow, array overruns, jumps to non-existent addresses, divide by zero, and the like. It is ridiculous to use an exception to clean up the mess you left on the carpet because you were too lazy to allocate and initialize an array or load a resource.

The reason object-oriented programming is the preferred choice for flock-driven code development is that sheep don't need to know what they're chewing beyond the own cud. No one sheep has any idea what the others are doing and doesn't care. This process is very efficient at producing fertilizer and mutton, but not software. Friends, this is where bloatware comes from.

Just say NO to object-oriented programming.

There is no more poignant (or ironic) example of dysfunctional code development than the recent out-sourcing of source code by Microsoft® for Windows®. W8, W8, and W9β. It remains to be seen how W10 will work out.

Appendix E: 16-32-64-Bit Programming

There are only minor differences between 32-bit and 64-bit code: the size of the integers and addresses. The biggest differences are between 16-bit and 32-bit code. The most significant compatibility issues arise from the fact that 16-bit code will run on a 32-bit machine and 32-bit code will run on a 64-bit machine, but 16-bit code will not run on a 64-bit machine.

Of course, neither 32-bit nor 64-bit code will run on a 16-bit machine, but no one tries to do this, because time moves in one direction and all of the 16-bit machines are gone. The problem is all of the 16-bit code that's still around and the applications that depend on it. This is a particular problem with old VB code. The source code for the 16-bit code has been lost, is not available, or won't compile for 32-bit or 64-bit operation.

There are also ways of loading and accessing various resources that were hold over from the days of 16-bit machines and were supported in the 32-bit operating systems, but are not in the 64-bit operating systems. This means that, even if you could recompile the code, you couldn't use it in the same way. The entire structure of the application must be changed.

This same difficult transition occurred when moving from MSDOS® applications that wrote directly into the video memory to Windows® applications that produced visual effects only through API function calls. These MSDOS® applications required a complete re-write and not just a few changes here and there. To be sure, there was considerable reluctance to make this transition. Those who refused to do so fell by the wayside. Don't make the same mistake.

Just say NO to the dead-end methods introduced by Visual BASIC® when we were living in a 16-bit world.

Appendix F: Working with Very Long Path Names

Ordinarily you are limited to approximately 255 characters for the drive, path, and file name on the Windows® operating system. Although you can easily create file names much longer than this by nesting paths having long names, these may be very difficult to access. This problem is often discovered after dragging folders to the desktop, which may add considerable length to the complete path name.

You may be able to see a file with Windows Explorer®, but when you double-click to open it, you get a message saying the file can't be found. Double-clicking on the file name may even crash or lock up an application, such as Acrobat® when opening a PDF document. Once you move or copy a folder, you may no longer be able to move, copy, or access the individual files in that folder. These problems arise from the file name length limitation built into countless programs as well as the operating system. There is a way around this that is virtually undocumented.

By now you should be aware that there are two versions of every API function that uses strings: Unicode and non-Unicode. Buried deep in obscurity beneath OpenFile() documentation lies the following nugget of information:

If [] is a path, there is a default string size limit of MAX_PATH characters. This limit is related to how the CreateFile() function parses paths. An application can transcend this limit and send in paths longer than MAX_PATH characters by calling the wide [Unicode] version of CreateFile() and prepending "\\?\" to the path. The "\\?\" tells the function to turn off path parsing; it lets paths longer than MAX_PATH be used with CreateFileW()... The "\\?\" is ignored as part of the path. For example, "\\?\C:\myworld\private" is seen as "C:\myworld\private"...

Most applications for the Windows® operating system don't utilize this feature and won't handle very long file and path names. Beyond Compare® is a file synchronizing utility of amazing utility from Scooter Software. Version 3 will handle these very long file and path names for you.

You must get Beyond Compare®–because it IS!

Appendix G: Painting with a Mask

Painting with Windows® is complicated by the fact that you can only perform operations within a *device context*. One common painting operation that is surprisingly difficult is painting with a mask. You may only want to paint parts of an image or the image may not be rectangular. In either case, you must apply a mask.

You could accomplish this by creating a mask, which must have a depth of 1 bit (i.e., B&W) and selecting this into one *device context*. Then selecting the image (which will most likely have a depth greater than 1 bit) into a second *device context*. Then calling MaskBlt() to perform the operation. Though tedious, this works well enough, unless what you're trying to paint is yet another bitmap in a third *device context*.

There is an easier way to accomplish this, which also eliminates the need to maintain two separate images (i.e., the picture and the mask). There are two undocumented API functions in wingdi.h that are particularly useful. These are: GdiTransparentBlt() and GdiGradientFill(). The first will paint anything but a single color. The second saves a lot of time if you want to implement a rainbow effect.

You can build the mask into the image itself by using some distinct color, as in the following:

Call GdiTransparentBlt() with the last parameter set to 0xFF00FF (i.e., magenta) and only the button will be drawn.

99

Appendix H: Put A Menu Wherever You Want It

Early versions of Windows® will only place a menu in a single location: at the top, below the caption. Later versions will place a menu in a few other specific locations, primarily to support languages that read from right-to-left and/or bottom-to-top. According to Microsoft® documentation, a child window can't have a menu, but this is not entirely accurate. You can't *create* a child window with a menu, because Windows® treats the 9th argument passed to CreateWindow() as the child ID rather than the handle to a menu.

You *can* create a child window with a menu and then put it wherever you want. First create a top-level window, passing it the handle of your menu. This will work, because it isn't a child window. Then call SetParent() to make the top-level menu a child of your main window. You'll also have to pass the messages to the main window procedure, because they will go to the parent of the menu, which is now a child window. Register a class named "MENU" and write a little procedure to send the messages along.

```
LRESULT WINAPI MenuProc(HWND hWnd,UINT wMsg,WPARAM
    wParam,LPARAM lParam)
{
if(wMsg==WM_CLOSE)
   return(FALSE);
if(wMsg==WM_COMMAND)
   {
   wParam&=0x0000FFFF;
   wParam|=((DWORD)BN_CLICKED)<<16;
   PostMessage(hMain,WM_COMMAND,wParam,0);
   return(FALSE);
   }
if(wMsg==WM_CREATE)
   return(FALSE);
return(DefWindowProc(hWnd,wMsg,wParam,lParam));
}
```

101

Appendix I: Click Here to Do Something Special

VB developers are accustomed to clicking on any object and having it do something special. When you click on almost anything in the Visual BASIC® development system, it creates a little function and shifts the developer's focus to that new function, where you can define that *special something* you want it to do. This is a useful behavior, but very misleading.

This is not *the way Windows® works!*

Clicking on a control only generates a message. This action doesn't call a function. Windows® simply posts one or more messages to the active queue. Different types of controls post different messages when you click on them. Some of those messages are associated with the handle of the control and some aren't.

In some cases, all you know is that the user clicked the mouse. In these cases you must figure out what the user clicked from the location of the cursor when the mouse was clicked and which controls were visible at that time. The position and visibility of controls may change between the time the message was posted and the time your application gets around to processing it.

If you want a function to be called when the user clicks on a control, you must watch for the message and then call the associated function. Windows® does not *do this for you.*

Watching for the message is also complicated by the fact that Windows® sends messages to the parent of a control. If the control is inside a GROUP box, which is inside a TAB control, your application loop won't see the message, because it's the great-grandparent. If you want this functionality, you must also provide some way of associating the function you want called with the message that is posted when the user clicks on that particular object.

The following code snippet illustrates creating and filling a DROPDOWN list and calling a function when the user selects something:

```
/* user-defined function to call when DROPDOWN is
   selected */
LRESULT WINAPI MyFunction(HWND hWnd,UINT wMsg,WPARAM
   wParam,LPARAM lParam)
   {
   my_selection=lParam;
   return(FALSE);
   }

/* create and fill the control before entering message
   loop */
char**selections;
hMine=CreateWindow("COMBOBOX",NULL,WS_CHILD|
   WS_VISIBLE|WS_CLIPSIBLINGS|CBS_DROPDOWNLIST|
```

```
         CBS_HASSTRINGS|WS_VSCROLL,left,top,wide,high,
         hParent,(HMENU)ID,hInst,NULL);
    SetWindowLong(hMine,GWL_USERDATA,(LONG)MyFunction);
    for(i=0;selections[i];i++)
      SendMessage(hMine,CB_ADDSTRING,0,
      (LPARAM)selections[i]);
    SendMessage(hMine,CB_SETCURSEL,0,0);

 /* inside message loop watch for message and call
    function */
    if((HWND)lParam==hMine)
      if(HIWORD(wParam)==CBN_SELCHANGE||
      HIWORD(wParam)==CBN_SELENDOK)
        if((wndproc=(WNDPROC)GetWindowLong((HWND)lParam,
      GWL_USERDATA))!=NULL)
          CallWindowProc(wndproc,(HWND)lParam,
      HIWORD(wParam),(WPARAM)GetWindowLong((HWND)lParam,
      GWL_ID),(LPARAM)SendMessage((HWND)lParam,
      CB_GETCURSEL,0,0));
```

Appendix J: BITMAPs with 32 Bits/Pixel

The problem with 32 bits/pixel BITMAPs is that Windows® doesn't recognize the corresponding file format. Pixel colors are stored as three bytes, ordered: blue, green, red. In 32 bits/pixel there's an extra byte after each triplet that isn't used for anything. Some displays use 32 bits/pixel because it's faster to access memory in 4-byte words than 3-byte triplets. If you have a 32 bits/pixel bitmap, you must convert it to 24 bits/pixel before saving it. The following code snippet will accomplish this:

```
void BMP32to24(BITMAPINFOHEADER*bm)
{
int h,i,j,w,w24,w32;
BYTE*bi;
w32=4*((bm->biWidth*32+31)/32);
w24=4*((bm->biWidth*24+31)/32);
bm->biCompression=0;
bm->biBitCount=24;
bm->biSizeImage=w24*bm->biHeight;
bi=((BYTE*)bm)+sizeof(BITMAPINFOHEADER);
for(h=0;h<bm->biHeight;h++)
   for(i=w32*h,j=w24*h,w=0;w<bm->biWidth;w++,i++)
      {
      bi[j++]=bi[i++];
      bi[j++]=bi[i++];
      bi[j++]=bi[i++];
      }
}
```

Appendix K: Using Command Line Parameters

Many Windows® programmers don't realize that commands can be passed to a GUI application just as they are to a command line application (or what's often called a DOS® application, but is actually a Win32® console application). This is how Excel® knows what to open when you double-click on a file. In that case Windows Explorer® passes the name of the file (including the complete path) to Excel® as a command line parameter.

Windows® GUIs begin with the function WinMain() which has four arguments: 1) this instance, 2) a previous instance (if applicable), 3) a pointer to the command line (not parsed), and 4) the show state of the window. Console applications (commonly–and erroneously–referred to as DOS® box) begin with the function main(), which has three arguments: 1) the number of command line parameters plus one (the extra [0] being the named of the program), 2) a pointer to a parsed list of command line parameters, and 3) a pointer to a parsed list of environment strings.

It can be tedious to parse the command line into strings, especially when there are quotation marks and paths containing spaces. This is not necessary. By the time the flow of program execution arrives at WinMain(), the O/S has already done this and put the results in three global parameters that correspond to the arguments passed to main(). These are:

```
int main(int argc,char**argv,char**envp);

extern int __argc;
extern char**__argv;
extern char**_environ;

int WINAPI WinMain(HINSTANCE hInstance,HINSTANCE
    hPrevInst,char*lpszLine,int nShow);
```

Appendix L: To GUI or Not To GUI

Many Windows® programmers don't realize that the same application can function with a GUI or command line interface without changing the code or recompiling. A command line interface is often–and erroneously–referred to as DOS® box. A command line interface is actually a Win32® console application. Your code will begin execution with WinMain(). If you want a GUI, register one set of classes and create one set of windows. If you want a console, register another set of classes and create another set of windows. Then call the AllocateConsole() function, as illustrated below:

```
HANDLE stdInput;
HANDLE stdOutput;
HWND hText;

void prints(char*format,...)/*call just like printf()*/
  {
  char bufr[128];
  DWORD l;
  va_list arg_marker;
  va_start(arg_marker,format);
  vsprintf(bufr,format,arg_marker);
  if(stdOutput)
     {
     strcat(bufr,"\r\n");
     WriteConsole(stdOutput,bufr,(DWORD)strlen(bufr),
     &l,NULL);
     }
  else
     SendMessage(hText,LB_ADDSTRING,0,(LPARAM)bufr);
  }

int WINAPI WinMain(...)
  {
  if(want_console)
     {
     AllocConsole();
     stdOutput=GetStdHandle(STD_OUTPUT_HANDLE);
     stdInput=GetStdHandle(STD_INPUT_HANDLE);
     RegisterClasses(FALSE);
     CreateWindows(FALSE);
     }
  else
     {
     RegisterClasses(TRUE);
     CreateWindows(TRUE);
     }
  while(GetMessage(&wMsg,NULL,0,0))
     {
```

109

```
        TranslateMessage(&wMsg);
        DispatchMessage(&wMsg);
        }
    return((int)wMsg.wParam);
    }
```

Appendix M: Manually Loading a DLL

There are situations when you must manually load a DLL, for instance, when you don't have a corresponding .LIB to link your application with or some licensure requirement. The following code snippet illustrates how to accomplish this:

```
typedef void  (__stdcall*CLOSECHANNEL)(int);
typedef void  (__stdcall*VALIDATE    )(char*);
typedef int   (__stdcall*DOCOMMAND    )(int,BYTE,
    BYTE,BYTE*,BYTE,int,BYTE*);
typedef int   (__stdcall*OPENCHANNEL )(short);

HINSTANCE     hi;
CLOSECHANNEL  CloseChannel;
DOCOMMAND     DoCommand;
OPENCHANNEL   OpenChannel;
VALIDATE      Validate;

void GetProcedures()
  {
  hi=LoadLibrary("Library.dll");
  Validate    =(Validate)
    GetProcAddress(hi,"Validate");
  OpenChannel =(OpenChannel)
    GetProcAddress(hi,"OpenChannel");
  CloseChannel=(CloseChannel)
    GetProcAddress(hi,"CloseChannel");
  DoCommand   =(DoCommand)
    GetProcAddress(hi,"DoCommand");
  }

int main(int argc,char**argv,char**envp)
  {
  short channel,port=1;
  GetProcedures();
  Validate(license);
  channel=OpenChannel(port);
  DoCommand(channel,byCmd,byQOS,pbyData,
    byLen,uiAppKey,byUniqueID);
  CloseChannel(channel);
  return(0);
  }
```

Appendix N: Painting without Flicker

You may want to paint a moving object on the display, for instance, an animation, such as a screen saver. If you implement this using the various GDI function calls, this will result in an annoying flicker effect. This can also happen when application windows are updated. In order to eliminate the flicker effect, you must paint the entire area with a single operation.

The various GDI functions, such as drawing lines and filling polygons, build the image on the display in a sequence of queued updates. In order to eliminate the flicker effect, you must separate the queued updates from the display, which means building the image in memory before painting it in a single operation. It will also help to paint only that portion of the new image that is different from the existing one.

To implement this process, you must create a compatible device context in memory as well as a DIB section and select this into the memory device context. Build the new image in memory, then use the BitBlt() function to paint it in single operation. The following code snippet illustrates how to accomplish this:

```
HBITMAP mBM;    /* memory bitmap */
HDC     mDC;    /* memory device contex */
HWND    hMain;  /* handle to application window */

void Render()
    {
    FillRect(mDC,&new,GetStockObject(BLACK_BRUSH));
    /* render image in memory device contex */
    }


TIMERPROC Animate(HWND hWnd,UINT uMsg,UINT idEvent,DWORD
    dwTime)
    {
    HDC hDC;
    Render();
    hDC=GetDC(hMain);
    BitBlt(hDC,left,top,wide,high,mDC,left,top,SRCCOPY);
    ReleaseDC(hMain,hDC);
    }


int WINAPI WinMain(...)
    {
    MSG wMsg;
    /* create the device contexts and DIB */
    hDC=GetDC(hMain);
    mDC=CreateCompatibleDC(hDC);
    ReleaseDC(hMain,hDC);
    bI.bmiHeader.biSize=sizeof(BITMAPINFOHEADER);
    bI.bmiHeader.biWidth=wide;
    bI.bmiHeader.biHeight=high;
```

113

```
bI.bmiHeader.biPlanes=1;
bI.bmiHeader.biBitCount=24;
bI.bmiHeader.biSizeImage=wide*high*3;

  mBM=CreateDIBSection(mDC,&bI,DIB_RGB_COLORS,&bits,NUL
  L,0);
SelectObject(mDC,mBM);
/* message loop */
SetTimer(hMain,1,1000,(TIMERPROC)Animate);
while(GetMessage(&wMsg,NULL,0,0))
   {
   TranslateMessage(&wMsg);
   DispatchMessage(&wMsg);
   }
return((int)wMsg.wParam);
}
```

Appendix O: Directory Walk

At some point you may want to find all of the files and folders on a disk or under a specific folder. This is called walking a directory. When you attempt this you may run into the very long path problem discussed in Appendix F. The following program performs a walk from the current directory all the way down, listing all of the files and folders beneath. It incorporates the method for handling very long path names presented in Appendix F.

```
#include <stdio.h>
#include <malloc.h>
#include <string.h>
#include <tchar.h>
#include <windows.h>

int files;
int npath;
int mpath;
wchar_t**Path;

int wstrlen(wchar_t*string)
  {
  char*ptr;
  int l;
  ptr=(char*)string;
  l=0;
  while(*ptr)
    {
    l++;
    ptr+=2;
    }
  return(l);
  }

wchar_t*wstrdup(wchar_t*string)
  {
  wchar_t*ptr;
  int l;
  l=wstrlen(string);
  ptr=calloc(l+1,sizeof(wchar_t));
  memcpy(ptr,string,(l+1)*sizeof(wchar_t));
  return(ptr);
  }

int wstrcmp(wchar_t*string1,wchar_t*string2)
  {
  char*ptr1,*ptr2;
  ptr1=(char*)string1;
  ptr2=(char*)string2;
  while(*ptr1||*ptr2)
```

115

```
  {
  if(*ptr1!=*ptr2)
    return(1);
  ptr1+=2;
  ptr2+=2;
  }
return(0);
}

wchar_t*wstrcpy(wchar_t*string1,wchar_t*string2)
  {
  int l;
  l=wstrlen(string2);
  memcpy(string1,string2,(l+1)*sizeof(wchar_t));
  return(string1);
  }

wchar_t*wstrcat(wchar_t*string1,wchar_t*string2)
  {
  int l1,l2;
  l1=wstrlen(string1);
  l2=wstrlen(string2);
  memcpy(string1+l1,string2,(l2+1)*sizeof(wchar_t));
  return(string1);
  }

char wprint(wchar_t*string)
  {
  char c,*ptr;
  ptr=(char*)string;
  while(*ptr)
    {
    c=*ptr;
    if(c==',')
      printf("%s","%2C");
    else
      printf("%c",c);
    ptr+=2;
    }
  return(c);
  }

wchar_t filename[8096];

wchar_t*BuildFileName(wchar_t*wname)
  {
  int i;
  wstrcpy(filename,L"\\\\?\\");
  for(i=0;i<npath;i++)
```

116

```
      {
   wstrcat(filename,Path[i]);
   if(wstrcmp(&Path[i][wstrlen(Path[i])-1],L"\\"))
      wstrcat(filename,L"\\");
      }
   wstrcat(filename,wname);
   return(filename);
   }

void FileDate(FILETIME fT)
   {
   int month,day,year,hour,minute,second;
   WORD date,time;
   FileTimeToDosDateTime(&fT,&date,&time);
   hour=time>>11;
   minute=(time&0x07E0)>>5;
   second=(time&0x001F)<<1;
   month=(date&0x01E0)>>5;
   day=(date&0x001F);
   year=(date>>9)+1980;
   printf("%02i/%02i/%04i
     %02i:%02i:%02i",month,day,year,hour,minute,second);
   }

void FileSize(DWORD hi,DWORD lo)
   {
   union{DWORD d[2];__int64 l;}u;
   u.d[0]=lo;
   u.d[1]=hi;
   printf("%6lld",u.l);
   }

void ListFile(WIN32_FIND_DATAW*wFind)
   {
   FileDate(wFind->ftLastWriteTime);
   printf(" ");
   FileSize(wFind->nFileSizeHigh,wFind->nFileSizeLow);
   printf(" 0x%04lX ",wFind->dwFileAttributes);
   wprint(BuildFileName(wFind->cFileName)+4);
   printf("\n");
   }

void ListAllFiles()
   {
   HANDLE hFind;
   WIN32_FIND_DATAW wFind;

   if((hFind=FindFirstFileW(BuildFileName(L"*.*"),&wFind
   ))==INVALID_HANDLE_VALUE)
```

117

```
        {
        npath--;
        return;
        }
  do{
        if(wstrcmp(wFind.cFileName,L".")==0)
          continue;
        if(wstrcmp(wFind.cFileName,L"..")==0)
          continue;
        if(wFind.dwFileAttributes&FILE_ATTRIBUTE_DIRECTORY)
          {
          ListFile(&wFind);
          Path[npath++]=wstrdup(wFind.cFileName);
          ListAllFiles();
          continue;
          }
        ListFile(&wFind);
        files++;
        }while(FindNextFileW(hFind,&wFind));
  FindClose(hFind);
  npath--;
  }

int main(int argc,char**argv,char**envp)
  {
  wchar_t*root;
  int l;
  l=GetCurrentDirectoryW(0,NULL);
  root=calloc(l,sizeof(wchar_t));
  GetCurrentDirectoryW(l,root);
  mpath=1000;
  Path=calloc(mpath,sizeof(wchar_t*));
  Path[0]=root;
  npath=1;
  printf("mm/dd/yyyy hh:mm:ss   size attrib name\n");
  ListAllFiles();
  printf("%i files found\n",files);
  return(0);
  }
```

Conclusion: Attention to Detail Matters

Someone who has only programmed in BASIC and never in assembler may be completely unaware of the machine instructions that their code ultimately becomes. Processors step through code one instruction at a time. It matters what you tell them to do. If you want to write high performance software, you must pay attention to detail. Consider the following four versions of what is nominally the same function:

```
double Resist1(double T)
{
double A0,A1,A2,A3;
A0=1.4821055E-3;
A1=2.3334343E-4;
A2=5.6284544E-7;
A3=8.0416136E-8;
return(A0+A1*T+A2*pow(T,2),+A3*pow(T,3));
}

double Resist2(double T)
{
double A0=1.4821055E-3,A1=2.3334343E-4,A2=5.6284544E-
   7,A3=8.0416136E-8;
return(((A3*T+A2)*T+A1)*T+A0);
}

double Resist3(double T)
{
static double A0=1.4821055E-3,A1=2.3334343E-
   4,A2=5.6284544E-7,A3=8.0416136E-8;
return(((A3*T+A2)*T+A1)*T+A0);
}

double Resist4(double T)
{
return(((8.0416136E-8*T+5.6284544E-7)*T+2.3334343E-
   4)*T+1.4821055E-3);
}
```

An optimizing compiler will never be able to replace such laziness as the use of pow() in the first example above. Converting this calculation to what is called Horner's method, as in the latter three examples, reduces the run time by 60%. What you may not appreciate is the subtle differences between these latter three examples.

For instance, it might surprise you to discover that the second and fourth differ by only 4% and that the fourth takes longer than the second. The third is the fastest of all, with another 10% reduction in time. The reason for the differences is the time it takes to move data back-and-forth.

119

In examples 1, 2, and 4, the constants (i.e., 1.4821055E-3) must be copied from global memory to local memory (from the code segment to the stack segment) before being loaded onto the FPU. In example 3 the values stay in the same place (the data segment) and are loaded directly onto the FPU.

Attention to detail really does matter!

also by D. James Benton

3D Articulation: Using OpenGL, ISBN-9798596362480, Amazon, 2021 (book 3 in the 3D series).

3D Models in Motion Using OpenGL, ISBN-9798652987701, Amazon, 2020 (book 2 in the 3D series.

3D Rendering in Windows: How to display three-dimensional objects in Windows with and without OpenGL, ISBN-9781520339610, Amazon, 2016 (book 1 in the 3D series).

A Synergy of Short Stories: The whole may be greater than the sum of the parts, ISBN-9781520340319, Amazon, 2016.

Azeotropes: Behavior and Application, ISBN-9798609748997, Amazon, 2020.

bat-Elohim: Book 3 in the Little Star Trilogy, ISBN-9781686148682, Amazon, 2019.

Boilers: Performance and Testing, ISBN: 9798789062517, Amazon 2021.

Combined 3D Rendering Series: 3D Rendering in Windows®, 3D Models in Motion, and 3D Articulation, ISBN-9798484417032, Amazon, 2021.

Complex Variables: Practical Applications, ISBN-9781794250437, Amazon, 2019.

Compression & Encryption: Algorithms & Software, ISBN-9781081008826, Amazon, 2019.

Computational Fluid Dynamics: an Overview of Methods, ISBN-9781672393775, Amazon, 2019.

Computer Simulation of Power Systems: Programming Strategies and Practical Examples, ISBN-9781696218184, Amazon, 2019.

Contaminant Transport: A Numerical Approach, ISBN-9798461733216, Amazon, 2021.

CPUnleashed! Tapping Processor Speed, ISBN-9798421420361, Amazon, 2022.

Curve-Fitting: The Science and Art of Approximation, ISBN-9781520339542, Amazon, 2016.

Death by Tie: It was the best of ties. It was the worst of ties. It's what got him killed., ISBN-9798398745931, Amazon, 2023.

Differential Equations: Numerical Methods for Solving, ISBN-9781983004162, Amazon, 2018.

Equations of State: A Graphical Comparison, ISBN-9798843139520, Amazon, 2022.

Evaporative Cooling: The Science of Beating the Heat, ISBN-9781520913346, Amazon, 2017.

Forecasting: Extrapolation and Projection, ISBN-9798394019494, Amazon 2023.

Heat Engines: Thermodynamics, Cycles, & Performance Curves, ISBN-9798486886836, Amazon, 2021.

Heat Exchangers: Performance Prediction & Evaluation, ISBN-9781973589327, Amazon, 2017.

Heat Recovery Steam Generators: Thermal Design and Testing, ISBN-9781691029365, Amazon, 2019.

Heat Transfer: Heat Exchangers, Heat Recovery Steam Generators, & Cooling Towers, ISBN-9798487417831, Amazon, 2021.

Heat Transfer Examples: Practical Problems Solved, ISBN-9798390610763, Amazon, 2023.

The Kick-Start Murders: Visualize revenge, ISBN-9798759083375, Amazon, 2021.

Jamie2: Innocence is easily lost and cannot be restored, ISBN-9781520339375, Amazon, 2016-18.

Kyle Cooper Mysteries: Kick Start, Monte Carlo, and Waterfront Murders, ISBN-9798829365943, Amazon, 2022.

The Last Seraph: Sequel to Little Star, ISBN-9781726802253, Amazon, 2018.

Little Star: God doesn't do things the way we expect Him to. He's better than that! ISBN-9781520338903, Amazon, 2015-17.

Living Math: Seeing mathematics in every day life (and appreciating it more too), ISBN-9781520336992, Amazon, 2016.

Lost Cause: If only history could be changed..., ISBN-9781521173770, Amazon, 2017.

Mass Transfer: Diffusion & Convection, ISBN-9798702403106, Amazon, 2021.

Mill Town Destiny: The Hand of Providence brought them together to rescue the mill, the town, and each other, ISBN-9781520864679, Amazon, 2017.

Monte Carlo Murders: Who Killed Who and Why, ISBN-9798829341848, Amazon, 2022.

Monte Carlo Simulation: The Art of Random Process Characterization, ISBN-9781980577874, Amazon, 2018.

Nonlinear Equations: Numerical Methods for Solving, ISBN-9781717767318, Amazon, 2018.

Numerical Calculus: Differentiation and Integration, ISBN-9781980680901, Amazon, 2018.

Numerical Methods: Nonlinear Equations, Numerical Calculus, & Differential Equations, ISBN-9798486246845, Amazon, 2021.

Orthogonal Functions: The Many Uses of, ISBN-9781719876162, Amazon, 2018.

Overwhelming Evidence: A Pilgrimage, ISBN-9798515642211, Amazon, 2021.

Particle Tracking: Computational Strategies and Diverse Examples, ISBN-9781692512651, Amazon, 2019.

Plumes: Delineation & Transport, ISBN-9781702292771, Amazon, 2019.

Power Plant Performance Curves: for Testing and Dispatch, ISBN-9798640192698, Amazon, 2020.

Practical Linear Algebra: Principles & Software, ISBN-9798860910584, Amazon, 2023.

Props, Fans, & Pumps: Design & Performance, ISBN-9798645391195, Amazon, 2020.

Remediation: Contaminant Transport, Particle Tracking, & Plumes, ISBN-9798485651190, Amazon, 2021.

ROFL: Rolling on the Floor Laughing, ISBN-9781973300007, Amazon, 2017.

Seminole Rain: You don't choose destiny. It chooses you, ISBN-9798668502196, Amazon, 2020.

Septillionth: 1 in 10^{24}, ISBN-9798410762472, Amazon, 2022.

Software Development: Targeted Applications, ISBN-9798850653989, Amazon, 2023.

Software Recipes: Proven Tools, ISBN-9798815229556, Amazon, 2022.

Steam 2020: to 150 GPa and 6000 K, ISBN-9798634643830, Amazon, 2020.

Thermochemical Reactions: Numerical Solutions, ISBN-9781073417872, Amazon, 2019.

Thermodynamic and Transport Properties of Fluids, ISBN-9781092120845, Amazon, 2019.

Thermodynamic Cycles: Effective Modeling Strategies for Software Development, ISBN-9781070934372, Amazon, 2019.

Thermodynamics - Theory & Practice: The science of energy and power, ISBN-9781520339795, Amazon, 2016.

The Waterfront Murders: As you sow, so shall you reap, ISBN-9798611314500, Amazon, 2020.

Weather Data: Where To Get It and How To Process It, ISBN-9798868037894, Amazon, 2023.